Critical Guides to French Texts

137 La Mort le roi Artu

Critical Guides to French Texts

EDITED BY ROGER LITTLE, †WOLFGANG VAN EMDEN, DAVID WILLIAMS

La Mort le roi Artu

Karen Pratt

Senior Lecturer in French
King's College London

London
Grant & Cutler Ltd 2004

© Grant & Cutler Ltd 2004

ISBN 0 7293 0444 2

DEPÓSITO LEGAL: V: 2.728 - 2004

Printed in Spain by
Artes Gráficas Soler, S.L., Valencia
for
GRANT & CUTLER LTD
55–57 GREAT MARLBOROUGH STREET, LONDON W1F 7AY

Contents

Preface		7
1.	Rewriting Arthurian Tradition: the context	9
2.	The Tragedy of Arthur's Death: the characters and the plot	26
3.	Interpreting Arthurian History: the quest for meaning	47
4.	Arthurian Values: condemnation or commemoration?	67
5.	The Art of the Prose Romancer	86
6.	Conclusion	102
Bibliography		103

Preface

Although this book is primarily a study of *La Mort le roi Artu*, the work's status as the final branch of a cyclic romance necessitates frequent allusion to its literary context. Within my text italicized numbers in brackets refer to the bibliography at the end of this volume; reference to the three core parts of the cycle will take the following form:

1. *Lancelot: roman en prose du XIIIe siècle*, ed. Alexandre Micha, TLF, 9 vols (Geneva: Droz, 1978–83) — chapter and paragraph reference.
2. *La Queste del Saint Graal*, ed. Albert Pauphilet, CFMA (Paris: Champion, 1923) — page reference.
3. *La Mort le roi Artu*, ed. Jean Frappier, 3rd edn, TLF 58 (Geneva: Droz/Paris: Minard, 1964) — paragraph and line reference.

The assumption underlying this study is that students have read the *Mort Artu*, but are willing to be challenged into a closer, more nuanced re-reading. I have attempted to provide a balanced account of scholarly opinion while nevertheless offering a divergent, personal reading of this most fascinating and ambiguous text. I have benefited enormously from the constructive responses and criticisms of Simon Gaunt, Elspeth Kennedy and especially of the late Wolfgang van Emden, who as ever gave selflessly of his time and whose encouragement and friendship are greatly missed.

This 'little blue book' is dedicated to the generations of students at Goldsmiths' and King's Colleges in London who have opted for medieval literature with enthusiasm, and especially to the King's undergraduates with whom this monograph was piloted. Finally, I should like to mention, in a sad act of commemoration, two people whose lives were tragically cut short during the writing of this book: Jessica Lawrence, a fine student, who carefully commented on an early draft, and Don Fowler, classical scholar and dear friend, who first introduced me to the poetics of the labyrinth.

1. Rewriting Arthurian Tradition: the context

The thirteenth-century *Mort le roi Artu* (henceforth the *Mort*) with its universal themes and archetypal plot is as appealing to modern students as it was to its contemporary audience. A tale of adultery, incest, murder and war it narrates the end of the Arthurian world and the deaths of its most famous inhabitants: Arthur, Guinevere, Lance-lot and Gawain. While undergraduates frequently study the *Mort* as an independent romance, the surviving manuscript evidence suggests that it was conceived as the final branch of a cyclic prose romance, which scholars traditionally call the Vulgate Cycle or *Lancelot-Grail* cycle. Attention will therefore be paid in this chapter to the work's relationship with the other branches of the cycle and to the factors which conditioned its reception: audience expectations based on familiarity with Arthurian tradition and the manuscript context in which the *Mort* was normally read. Moreover, in order to evaluate its anonymous author's contribution to Arthurian literature, we shall explore the complex oral and written tradition he inherited and rewrote innovatively, most notably by linking Arthur's downfall with the adultery of Lancelot and Guinevere.

The Literary Context of the 'Mort Artu'

(N.B. most dates are approximate).
– Geoffrey of Monmouth, *Historia regum Britanniae* (*History of the Kings of Britain*), 1138
– Wace, *Roman de Brut* (vernacular translation of Geoffrey), 1155
– Chrétien de Troyes, *Erec et Enide*; *Cligés*; *Lancelot* or *Le Chevalier de la charrete*; *Yvain* or *Le Chevalier au lion*; *Perceval*, or *Le Conte du Graal*, 1170s–91
– Marie de France, *Lais* (including *Lanval*), 1180s
– Beroul, *Tristran*, 2nd half 12th century

- Continuations of Chrétien's *Perceval*, late 12th and early 13th centuries
- Robert de Boron, *Roman de l'estoire dou Graal* (or *Joseph*) and *Merlin*, 1200
- Anon, *Lancelot do Lac*, early 13th-century non-cyclic prose romance
- Prose cycle of Robert de Boron's works, including *Didot Perceval* (which ends on a *Mort Artu* narrative), early 13th century
- Vulgate Cycle or *Lancelot-Grail* Cycle: *Estoire du Saint Graal, Merlin, Suite du Merlin, Lancelot** proper, *Queste**, *Mort** (the three core branches asterisked here constituting the *Prose Lancelot*), 1215–35 (for whole cycle).

The legend of King Arthur began its life in the dark ages in the form of oral stories about a sixth-century warlord. In the next few centuries Arthur and his battles are mentioned in Latin chronicles, and Arthurian characters feature in Celtic tales. However, in the twelfth century this predominantly oral material was transformed by clerks into full-length written narratives designed to entertain and to instruct medieval audiences. Geoffrey of Monmouth's *Historia regum Britanniae*, a pseudo-historical chronicle in Latin prose on the kings of Britain, provided the Middle Ages with the first biography of the man whom Geoffrey considered the greatest British king (22, pp.205–61). Beginning with Arthur's conception (aided by the magic of Merlin), Geoffrey describes Arthur's meteoric rise at the age of 15 to the throne of Britain, his various successful campaigns against the kingdom's foes and his conquests abroad. The king's demise is the result of the treachery of his nephew, Mordred, the queen's lover. Arthur is presented as an active, just, courageous Christian ruler, whose exemplary chivalry and courtesy attract knights from Britain and abroad to attend his court. By the time of Geoffrey some characters had already become established Arthurian figures: Gawain, his favourite nephew, characterised by his prowess and epic boasting; Kay, Arthur's seneschal; and the

Rewriting Arthurian Tradition: the context 11

adulterous Queen Guinevere, who eventually repents and ends her days as a nun.

Geoffrey's popular *Historia* reached an even wider audience through Wace's Anglo-Norman verse translation entitled the *Roman de Brut*. Wace, a Norman cleric, preserved the broad outlines of Geoffrey's account, but added material (including the first reference to the Round Table) and explained or elaborated upon his Latin source. One addition by the adaptor is Gawain's lengthy speech responding to the claim by an older knight that peacetime activities, including frivolous lovemaking, can produce a loss of valour in young knights (*24*, ll.1911–46). Gawain argues, however, that a knight committing acts of chivalry in order to win a lady's love increases in prowess, thereby enhancing his own and his lady's reputation. Amplifying an idea already in Geoffrey (*22*, pp.229–30), Wace here offers a clear example of the chivalry topos (or commonplace), whereby love and prowess are seen in a symbiotic relationship (see *82*, p.13; *Mort*, 7:8–10; 25:36–45). Later, noting the absence of any reference to Arthur's progeny in the *Historia*, Wace explicitly states that Arthur and Guinevere could not have children, despite the king's love for his wife (*24*, ll.960–62). He also implies that although Guinevere sincerely repents of her actions, she does willingly share Mordred's bed (*24*, ll.4363–82), rendering more explicit hints made by Geoffrey (*22*, pp.257–59).

The idea of Guinevere's unfaithful nature is also present in *Lanval*, a *lai* by Marie de France, but it is Chrétien de Troyes's *Chevalier de la charrete* or *Lancelot* that first depicts the queen's adulterous relationship with Lancelot. This liaison has obvious repercussions for our view of King Arthur. In Chrétien's early romances, *Erec et Enide* and *Cligés*, Arthur is presented as an active and exemplary monarch, who attracts fine knights to his court, where they learn the *courtoisie*, prowess, *largesse* (generosity) and a sense of justice for which he is renowned (see *141*). In the *Charrete*, however, Arthur is ineffectual when faced with a challenger, Meléagant, who taunts the king with news of his subjects imprisoned in a foreign land. Unable to rescue them himself, Arthur grants a rash promise to Kay, who fails to defend

Guinevere in combat, and the queen is thus abducted by Meléagant. Rescue attempts are left to Gawain and an unnamed, mysterious knight, later identified as Lancelot. He succeeds in liberating Guinevere and the prisoners, and is rewarded with a night of love with the queen, Arthur thereby being cuckolded. The influence of the Tristan legend is obvious, though Chrétien, unlike the authors of *Tristan* romances and the *Mort*, avoids any direct confrontation between the heroine's husband and her lover by allowing the adultery to take place in an ill-defined, dream-like Celtic Other World. Nevertheless, Arthur's reputation as ideal king and husband is tarnished by this romance. Similarly, Gawain's reputation is compromised as the greatest of Arthur's knights. Being the favoured nephew, he was traditionally expected to succeed Arthur in the absence of a direct heir. However, in the *Charrete*, Gawain fails in his quest to rescue Guinevere, not because of any flaw in his character or any chivalric inadequacy, but because Lancelot's prowess is greater for being inspired by love. The *Charrete* thus paves the way for the eclipsing of Gawain by Lancelot in the Vulgate Cycle.

While there is some ambiguity and possible irony in the treatment of love in Chrétien's work, in the early 13th-century non-cyclic prose romance, *Lancelot do Lac* (23), Lancelot appears as the greatest exponent of the chivalry topos. He is ennobled by love and the queen's reputation is similarly enhanced by the exploits of her *chevalier servant*. Love inspires Lancelot's beneficial acts of chivalry and his evolution towards perfection, culminating in his acceptance as the most illustrious companion of the Round Table. The hero's greater allegiance to Guinevere than to Arthur is carefully justified in this romance, for Arthur, having failed to avenge the death of Lancelot's father, does not gird on the young knight's sword during his dubbing, an act performed later by the queen herself. This detail averts any criticism of our hero on feudal grounds, for Lancelot is not strictly speaking Arthur's vassal and therefore his love for the queen is not treasonous. Nor is it suggested at this stage that human passion is an obstacle to the chivalric or moral progress of the knight. The idea that Lancelot's love for

Rewriting Arthurian Tradition: the context

Guinevere will prevent him from achieving perfection is not introduced into Arthurian tradition until the non-cyclic account of Lancelot's childhood and early adventures is incorporated into the *Lancelot-Grail* cycle. The non-cyclic *Lancelot* contains allusions to a Grail quest, but one already completed by Perceval (see *91*, Chapter VI).

Perceval as Grail seeker would have been known to audiences through Chrétien de Troyes's unfinished *Conte del Graal* or *Perceval*. Here too the eponymous hero eclipses Gawain and King Arthur appears weak and ineffectual. This incomplete romance gave rise to several verse continuations of the adventures of Perceval and Gawain. However, around 1200 a very different conception of the Grail was introduced by Robert de Boron's *Roman de l'estoire dou Graal*, otherwise known as the *Joseph* and part of a larger, fragmentary verse cycle. Robert transforms Chrétien's Celtico-Christian Grail into an unequivocally Christian relic associated with the life and passion of Christ: the vessel used by Christ at the Last Supper and later employed to collect his blood. In tracing the Grail back to biblical times Robert facilitated the insertion of secular Arthurian romance into the history of the Christianisation of the West and even into Salvation History (a Christian view of history whose major events are the Creation, Fall, Incarnation, Passion/Resurrection, Second Coming and Last Judgement, see *43*).

The early decades of the thirteenth century witnessed the birth of the great cyclical prose romances. The fashion began with whoever adapted Robert de Boron's verse cycle into prose. The result was a work containing a *Joseph* (based on Robert's *Roman de l'estoire dou Graal*), a *Merlin* (telling of Arthur's early life) and a *Perceval*. The latter (called the *Didot Perceval*) depicts Perceval's successful winning of the Grail and contains a short *Mort* section based on Wace, which makes no mention of Lancelot. In this work, Gawain replaces Perceval as the best knight at Arthur's court, and, the Grail adventures now completed, foreign campaigns are embarked upon, which enable Mordred to commit the treachery which brings about the end of Arthurian civilisation.

Shortly after the composition of this *Perceval-Grail* cycle someone decided to incorporate the non-cyclic *Lancelot do Lac* into a larger cycle, which now presented Lancelot's son Galahad (not Perceval) as the Grail winner (see *91*, Chapters X–XII). The core of this 'Vulgate' Cycle was the *Prose Lancelot* 'trilogy' made up of:

1. the *Lancelot* proper (Lancelot's early adventures and the consummation of his adulterous love);[1]
2. the *Queste del Saint Graal* (depicting Galahad's successful completion of the Grail adventures);
3. the *Mort* (narrating the demise of the cycle's two heroes: Arthur and Lancelot). Later authors, in an attempt to supply early histories for the Grail and Arthur, added to the beginning of the *Prose Lancelot* an *Estoire* and a *Merlin* (both ultimately based on Robert de Boron) and a *Merlin* continuation, thus creating an even larger *Lancelot-Grail* cycle. The hugely popular *Mort* survives in over 45 manuscripts, yet it rarely appears alone. Most often it occurs with the *Queste* and some or all of the *Lancelot* proper. On 8 occasions it is found in manuscripts containing the complete *Lancelot-Grail* cycle. Clearly its manuscript context conditioned the way the *Mort* was read.

Authorship and Dating of the 'Lancelot-Grail' Cycle

Although the texts constituting the *Prose Lancelot* were frequently copied and consequently read together, they were not necessarily composed by the same author. Indeed, critics are unanimous in their rejection of the Walter Map attribution, despite his being named in paragraphs 1 and 204 of the *Mort*, in the *Queste* (p.280), and in some manuscripts of the *Lancelot* proper (CVIII, 16). Walter, archdeacon of Oxford, friend of Henry II and author of some Latin exemplary tales, died around 1209, a date generally agreed to be too early for the *Prose Lancelot* (c.1215–30, but see *146*). His name was probably cited to give the work an air of authority.

---

[1] Although some critics refer to the *Lancelot* proper as the *Prose Lancelot*, I shall use the latter term to designate the three core branches of the *Lancelot-Grail* cycle.

Early scholarship was divided on the question of single or multiple authorship for the *Lancelot-Grail* cycle. Critics who argued for unity of composition and ethos in the whole cycle (excluding the *Merlin* and its *Suite*) claimed that minor discrepancies in the early branches had arisen because the *Estoire* was composed after the author had begun the *Lancelot* proper, but before he embarked on its *Charrete* episode. On the other hand, those who supported multiple authorship explained away any cohesion between the separate branches as the result of *remaniement*: interpolations and modifications made by later scribes and redactors (for a range of differing views, see *105*; *106*; *51*; *128*; *129*). Carman (*55*) incredibly postulated the participation of over a dozen writers working under the patronage of the abbey of Fontevrault and its daughter houses to produce a cycle reflecting the different emotional and spiritual stages in the life of Eleanor of Aquitaine, Henry II of England's wife!

Frappier's answer to the authorship debate was to suggest that one man, whom he calls the 'architect', devised the cycle's overall plan and probably composed the *Lancelot* proper (or the majority of it), but gave the *Queste* and *Mort* to other writers, whom he supervised (*66*). Noting the references to Meaux and to the feast of the Magdalen, Frappier agreed with Lot that the cycle was produced by clerics from the Champagne region (*2*, pp.viii–ix). More recently, Micha, stressing what he identifies as its 'inspiration religieuse', favours single authorship for the *Prose Lancelot* (*117*, p.306). It is our aim here to re-assess the religious spirit of the *Mort* and to challenge the idea that one ethos (emanating from a single author or supervising architect) unifies the three core branches of the cycle.

The Ethos of the 'Prose Lancelot'

Although the *Mort* always appears in cyclical manuscripts as a sequel to the *Queste*, the following textual summaries reveal that the *Mort* has more in common stylistically and ideologically with the *Lancelot* proper than with its immediate predecessor (see *64*, p.253; *41*, note 19). One of the fascinating challenges facing any reader of the *Mort* is to decide how far the Arthurian world's return to pre-quest secular values is being condemned by the author, that is how far the narrative encourages us to read it from the perspective of the *Queste*.

At the beginning of the *Lancelot* proper, where the non-cyclic romance's account of Lancelot's early life, love for Guinevere and friendship with Galeholt has been incorporated into the Vulgate Cycle, a positive view of the love affair is given. However, from the revised false Guinevere episode onwards, Lancelot's relationship with the queen starts to be more explicitly condemned (see *91*, Chapter X). There are hints that the adultery will prevent Lancelot from completing the adventures of the Grail, reserved for a virgin knight, and that Guinevere will be the cause of disasters, including the death of Lancelot's friend, Galeholt. This negative portrayal of the queen is reinforced by her growing lack of trust in Lancelot, evident when Morgan imprisons him and sends his ring to court (an episode preparing Guinevere's jealousy in the *Mort*). Arthur, on the other hand, is presented reasonably positively, and his unshakeable love for Lancelot (IX, 43) clearly implies nobility of heart. Yet the king's willing acceptance as his consort of a woman posing as Guinevere, for which the pope places his realm under an interdict, is a more negative trait. There is thus some ambiguity (or a realistic combination of good and bad qualities) in the portrayal of Arthur, as there is in the relationship between Lancelot and Guinevere (see *91*, p.264). For example, the Queen acknowledges that she is being punished for her sinful infidelity, yet believes that Lancelot and his prowess are worth it (IX, 1). Indeed, Lancelot's love for the queen enables him to rescue the knights imprisoned in the Val Sans Retor, his love-inspired chivalry still being viewed as socially beneficial at this stage in the cycle.

The Vulgate *Lancelot* proper includes a *Charrete* episode based on Chrétien, yet although in the prose retelling Lancelot, inspired by love, succeeds in rescuing Guinevere, he fails to rescue Symeu from his fiery grave because Lancelot has inherited his father's sinful state (XXXVII, 36–41). Indeed in the *version courte* (found in some manuscripts) Lancelot's own adultery is a further

Rewriting Arthurian Tradition: the context

impediment. The Symeu adventure, added by the Vulgate author to cast a shadow over Lancelot, is finally achieved by Galahad in the *Queste*. A more condemnatory tone is noticeable in the part of the *Lancelot* proper aptly called by Frappier the *Preparation for the Quest* (LIIIff.). Here Galahad is conceived in the Grail castle at Corbenic. Yet while the behaviour of Galahad's mother, the daughter of the Grail King Pellés, is presented as providential, Lancelot's misdirected passion (he thinks he is with Guinevere) is considered sinful. Lancelot is accorded a glimpse of the Grail, but as the *Lancelot* proper draws to a close its hero's limitations become more obvious and we sense that his worldly ideals are going to be eclipsed by those of his more spiritually motivated virgin son. However, as Frappier notes (*67*, p.302) there is ambiguity, a *double esprit*, in the treatment of chivalry and love throughout the *Lancelot* proper, which is not dispelled until the *Queste*. As we shall see, though, ambiguity returns in the *Mort*, thus rendering the interpretation of events challenging for both protagonists and readers.

The allegorical *Queste* is linked to the Vulgate *Lancelot* proper through opposition and a gradual undermining of the values of the earlier work, so that a new understanding of chivalry replaces the old (*91*, p.302). The companions of the Round Table set off on what they consider to be a quest for an object, the Grail. They discover, however, that their adventures are symbolic of an inner journey which leads, in the case of the three elect (Galahad, Perceval and Bohort) to a more intimate knowledge of God. The knights who approach these adventures with conventional prowess fail, while those who understand the spiritual significance of the various tests come closest to witnessing the mysteries of the Grail. Understanding is aided by a series of hermits who explain dreams, visions, the symbolic words and events which make up the knights' spiritual education. One such hermit attributes Lancelot's failure to his adultery with Guinevere (*Queste*, p.66), and advises him to adopt a life of chastity and humility. Another hermit interprets Gawain's allegorical dream as prophesying the success in the quest of Galahad, Perceval and Bohort (represented by pure or almost spotless bulls), but also the subsequent destruction of the Round Table because of the pride and lust of their companions (*Queste*, pp.155–57). Yet Gawain ignores any advice and makes less spiritual progress in this branch of the cycle than Lancelot. The latter's limited success is enhanced by the honour of being the father of Galahad, the virgin knight who heals the Maimed King with blood from the bleeding lance. Galahad is then crowned in the Holy Land, and after openly witnessing the mysteries of the Grail (perhaps by seeing the face of God, see *8*, p.304, note 87) dies in ecstasy. At this point the Grail and Lance are taken by a mysterious hand up to Heaven and never seen again. Perceval spends his last days as a religious in a hermitage, and after his pious death Bohort decides to return to Arthur's court to spread the good news of the Grail.

The Ethos of the 'Mort Artu': rewriting the sources

It is Bohort, clad in his secular clothes, who forms the narrative link between the moralising, didactic *Queste* and the more secular, dramatic *Mort*. Interestingly, paragraphs 1–3, which echo the *Queste*'s dénouement and which relate how Bohort returns to court to announce the passing of Galahad and Perceval, and how Gawain is questioned about the killing of 18 knights of the Round Table during the quest, are attached in some manuscripts to the end of the *Queste*, the scribes marking the beginning of the *Mort* at 3:38 (see *1*, pp.xi–xii). The scribal confusion over the exact boundaries between the final two branches and the sudden return to the ethos of the *Lancelot* proper after §4 of the *Mort* may indicate that a version of the *Mort* close to ours was in existence prior to the composition of the Vulgate *Queste* and was superficially reworked (mainly by adding some linking paragraphs) to form a sequel to it. Indeed, Sommer argues that at an earlier stage in the evolution of the prose romance cycles, the *Mort* (largely in its present form) constituted the final branch of a cycle with a Perceval quest (*10*, I, p.xv; VI, p.204). In that case the *Mort* would have finished off a less didactic and morally improving cycle than the Vulgate Cycle. Since, however, the extant manuscripts provide little evidence for Sommer's postulated intermediate stage, I shall assume, with some reservations, that the Vulgate *Mort* was conceived as a deliberate sequel (and response) to the Vulgate *Queste*.

The most important legacy of the *Queste* to the *Mort* is the idea that now the adventures of the Holy Grail have been completed there is little left for the Knights of the Round Table to achieve. This is mentioned in the *Mort* section of the *Didot Perceval* too (*21*, p.70), but in the Vulgate *Mort* Arthur attempts to fill the void by arranging, not a campaign against his enemies abroad, but the Winchester tournament (3:38–43). This is one of a series of tournaments designed either to keep the Knights of the Round Table in training or to attract Lancelot back to court. The renewed passion of Lancelot for Guinevere is then contrasted with the chaste behaviour shown in the *Queste*, whose ethos is still felt in the two references to the adulterous love as *pechié* (§4). However, the author of the *Mort* focuses less on moral issues than on Lancelot's infraction of the courtly convention of *bien celer* (discretion), which he had earlier practised in the *Lancelot* proper (LXXXIV, 28 and XXXVI, 36). Indeed, the consequences of his *folie* are sociopolitical rather than spiritual and the *Mort* thus reverts to the ethos of the *Lancelot* proper.

The early part of the *Mort* resembles a psychological romance, treating the lovers' relationship, attempts to trap them and the revelation of their adultery to Arthur. A primary source for this section is the *Lancelot* proper, from which the author adopts the theme of Guinevere's jealousy (then over the daughter of King Pellés (CV, 36–CVI, 5) and now over the demoiselle d'Escalot) and consequent rejection of Lancelot. Other motifs and episodes adapted or continued from the earlier branch include the queen's need for a champion (then to disprove the claims of the false Guinevere (VIII, 15), now against accusations of murder by Mador de la Porte (§62ff.)), Morgan's machinations and Lancelot's paintings (LXXXVI, 16–23), tournaments, quests for Lancelot (XXXIIIa–XLIIa), incognitos and woundings (LVII, 18: Lancelot wounded by a 'porc sauvage'). For the poisoned fruit episode three possible sources have been postulated: the early thirteenth-century *chansons de geste Gaydon* and *Parise la Duchesse* (see *69*, pp.196–98), and Geoffrey of Monmouth's *Vita Merlini* (see *134*). However, recent redating of the first two texts rules them out as sources and suggests that we are dealing with a popular motif exploited independently by several authors. As the relationship between Guinevere and her *chevalier servant* becomes more passionate, the influence of the *Tristan* legend is detectable (see *69*, pp.188–95; *125*). Agravain and Mordred behave rather like the evil barons in Beroul's romance (*13*), for they spy on the lovers, set traps for them, spread malicious gossip and their motives for telling the truth have little to do with a concern for the king's honour (5:2–4). Guinevere's treatment at the hands of the 'felon chevalier' (92:12), who lead her to the stake and 'li firent honte et laidure' (92:6), recalls the abuse suffered by Iseut (*Tristran*, 1073–74, 1141–54) and the concern expressed by the common people (93:35–37) echoes the *vox populi* of Beroul's romance. Moreover, Gawain's threat (93:17–26) to return his fief if the queen is burned parallels the attitude of Marc's seneschal, Dinas (*Tristran*, 1125–40). Though not presented quite as negatively as King Marc, Arthur is here shown at his most cruel and vengeful (92:37–39).

The events consequent upon Lancelot's rescue of the queen and the killing of Gawain's brothers seem to be of the prose romancer's own invention, although during the siege of Joyeuse Garde (104:108ff.) we are reminded of Lancelot's winning of the castle as narrated in the *Lancelot* proper (XXIVa). In this episode Lancelot is presented in a very magnanimous light when he allows Arthur's army to rest on arrival (109:1–8) and saves the king's life in the ensuing battle (§§115–16). The description of the lovers' parting and the queen's return to Arthur after the intervention of the pope (§§117–19) does, however, recall both Beroul's *Tristran* (2681–932) and the *Lancelot* proper (IX, 4ff.).

When Arthur, goaded on by Gawain's grief-ridden *desmesure*, pursues Lancelot to Gaunes, leaving Logres in the treacherous hands of Mordred, we find echoes of the story of Arthur's death as told by Geoffrey, by Wace and in the *Didot Perceval*. The author of the *Mort* was no slavish imitator of his sources though; they provided the material for his own innovative treatment. The accounts of Arthur's death in the *Historia* and *Brut* run as follows: after an expedition to

Rewriting Arthurian Tradition: the context

Gaul to fight Frollo (a possible source for Arthur's pursuit of Lancelot to Gaunes), the king celebrates his second coronation, during which a delegation from Rome claims tribute from the Britons. Arthur decides to challenge the Roman demands, leaves his nephew, Mordred, and Guinevere in charge of the kingdom, kills the giant of the Mont-Saint-Michel and eventually defeats the Romans at Saussy. After a winter has passed, he is ready to march on Rome when he hears of Mordred's treachery and incestuous adultery with the queen. (Sex with an aunt by marriage was considered to be incest, though none of the *Mort*'s sources makes this explicit.) Mordred, aided by many pagans, meets Arthur's army when it lands in Britain and Gawain is killed at Richborough. Mordred retreats to Winchester (in Wace he goes first to London then to Winchester) and Guinevere enters a nunnery. Two more battles ensue, at Winchester and on the banks of the Camblan, where Arthur attacks Mordred's squadron and his nephew is killed (though his killer is not identified). The king is mortally wounded and taken to Avalon. He is succeeded by his cousin Constantine, who fights Mordred's two sons when they challenge him. Eventually, Constan-tine kills them in sacrilegious circumstances.

According to Frappier (*69*, pp.152–72) the author of the *Mort* used Wace more than Geoffrey, but drew on the *Historia* for additional detail when he found the *Brut*'s account too compressed. He retains the reference to the regency of Mordred when Arthur goes abroad, but places this in a new context, just prior to Arthur's departure in pursuit of Lancelot (§129, cf. the *Didot Perceval*, *21*, p.71). Whereas Wace emphasises Mordred's illicit passion for Guinevere right from the beginning (2347–63), the *Mort* hints more subtly at Mordred's possible intentions (§129). Moreover, the queen is presented, not as a willing partner in the treachery, but as an excellent judge of character, who knows that the young man is disloyal and is therefore angry at being placed in his care (129:19–24). The old woman's speech (§131) announcing Gawain's imminent death evokes the prophetic vision, related in the *Lancelot* proper, in which Gawain while at Corbenic witnesses fighting between a leopard and a dragon: the latter kills and is killed by the baby dragons issued from its mouth (LXVI, 19–21). While Arthur is laying siege to Gaunes, *li contes* returns us to England, where Mordred's passion for the queen has been fuelled by living in close proximity to her (134:12–15, a detail which reveals the author's interest in psychology). The usurper's attempt to persuade everyone, by means of a false letter, that Arthur is dead and that it was his last wish that Mordred should succeed him and marry Guinevere, is an innovation that provides a splendid role for the queen in the *Mort*. Her plight reflects the vulnerability of royal widows in the Middle Ages, but she resists admirably, showing great loyalty to Arthur. Meanwhile, back in Gaunes, the conflict is resolved by a combat between Lancelot and Gawain (a doubling of the earlier *judicium Dei* or judgement of God fought by Mador de la Porte and Lancelot over the queen's guilt in the poisoned fruit affair, §§82ff.). The second combat affords another demonstration of Lancelot's magnanimity, for he spares Gawain's life. Nevertheless, a head-wound inflicted by Lancelot will eventually prove fatal. It is at this point that Arthur is informed that the Romans are invading Gaul. There is no council scene in the *Mort* to match those in its possible sources (though this motif has been transposed to an earlier point in the narrative, before the siege of Joyeuse Garde, §§103–04). Thus Arthur's barons have little control over events, while Gawain, confident in his fitness to fight, encourages the king to march against the Romans. The ensuing war is presented in abbreviated form in the Vulgate version. Whereas Geoffrey and Wace show Gawain in combat with Lucius, the Roman Procurator, in the *Mort* Gawain attacks the emperor and his nephew, killing the latter. As a result of Roman reprisals, Gawain's head-wound reopens. Arthur is explicitly given the honour of killing the emperor (cf. *Didot Perceval, 21*, p.88). However, any rejoicing at the Roman defeat is shortlived, since ironically on the very day of his victory Arthur receives news from Guinevere of Mordred's treachery (§163). Here the temporal compression intensifies the tragedy, for Geoffrey and Wace had given the king a winter to recover before receiving bad news from home. This modification in chronology may, however, have been suggested by the *Didot Perceval (21*, p.90).

Rewriting Arthurian Tradition: the context

For the author of the *Mort* Mordred's treachery fulfils the hermit's prophecy in the *Lancelot* (XCVI, 23), where Mordred is held responsible for Arthur's death and the destruction of the Round Table. Arthur's recollection of the dream he had the night Mordred was conceived, in which a serpent crawled out of his belly, set fire to his land and attacked him personally (cf. *Lancelot* proper, XCVI, 24) is strategically placed in §164 to remind the audience of Mordred's moral responsibility at a critical point in the *Mort* narrative.

Arthur's three battles against Mordred (narrated summarily by Wace and Geoffrey, who show greater enthusiasm for the Roman war), are combined into one epic, climactic battle on Salisbury Plain. Guinevere enters a convent as soon as Arthur arrives in England (§§169–70), and there is no fighting at the coast, though Gawain does die on arrival from the wound inflicted originally by Lancelot. In earlier accounts of the battle of Camblan, Arthur attacks his treacherous nephew, but it is not clear who is responsible for their deaths. In the *Mort*'s battle of Salisbury Plain Mordred is the aggressor, killed by his father, but not before fatally wounding him. The idea, first mentioned in Mordred's forged letter, that he is Arthur's illegitimate son, is a modification to Arthurian legend probably invented by the prose romancer, under the influence of a similar charge of incest against Charlemagne (see *114*; *72*); ambiguity on this point in the *Lancelot* proper could be due to later scribal interpolation (see Chapter 2). Clearly the final great battle has been rewritten in the *Mort* to intensify the tragedy of Arthur's end. This tragic atmosphere is further reinforced by Arthur's unintentional killing of Lucan (§192) and by references to the king's death, which contradict audience expectations based on Merlin's prophecy of Arthur's return in Wace (4439–58) and in oral legend. However, although the prose romancer gives his work a stronger sense of closure than his pseudo-historical predecessors, uncertainty concerning Arthur's death still remains. The work is called '*La Mort le Roi Artu*' (1:10), yet the narrator refers in the prologue only to the wounding of Arthur and to the fact that no-one after Girflet saw him alive. The combat between Mordred and the king is later summed up as follows: 'Einsi ocist li peres le fill, et le filz navra le pere a mort'

(191:1–2) as if the author were avoiding direct reference to Arthur's death. He follows his sources when he shows the mortally wounded king departing to Avalon with Morgan and other ladies (§193, see *69*, pp.172–74), but diverges from them in implying that, their healing powers having failed, Arthur's body is buried with Lucan in the Noire Chapele (§194). This event, however, is not depicted, but narrated to Girflet by a *preudome*; we, like Girflet, have to accept the fact of Arthur's death on trust. So, despite the claim in 1191 by the monks of Glastonbury that they had found Arthur's grave, the circumstances of his death in the *Mort* with its echoes of Christ's burial (see *75*, p.262, note 107) and of the Celtic *merveilleux* (193:30–47) raise doubts regarding the contents of Arthur's tomb.

Of greater import even than the king's death is the tragic end of the civilisation that bore his name, for, as Merlin prophesied, the battle of Salisbury leaves 'LI ROIAUMES DE LOGRES ... ORFELINS' (178:20–21). When Arthur asks for Excalibur, the symbol of his temporal power, to be thrown into the lake this implies not only that his reign is drawing to a close (193:7–8), but that he has no surviving blood heir. Again, there is a parallel with Charlemagne, who, in the *Karlamagnús saga*, throws Roland's sword Durendal into a stream (see *114*, p.369). However, in the *Mort* this gesture contains an element of hope, expressed in the king's prayer to Christ (192:34–38) that Lancelot du Lac be his successor and that Arthur should be given a sign of God's approval of this choice. His prayer is answered when a hand rises out of the lake and brandishes the sword, evocative of, but not necessarily the negative counterpart to, the hand which takes the Grail and Lance up to heaven at the end of the *Queste*. In accordance with Arthur's wishes it is Lancelot and his kin (not Constantine as in the sources) who avenge the king's death on Mordred's two sons. The latter are killed in the battle of Winchester, and Lancelot (unlike Arthur's cousin Constantine in the *Historia*, whose sacrilegious behaviour is punished by God) spends his remaining years serving the Lord. Here we have an echo of the tradition in the epic of revolt whereby the hero turns to religion in old age. It should be noted that the final interview between Lancelot and

Guinevere, printed in the appendix to Frappier's edition, is a scribal addition, not part of the romancer's original conception.

In retelling the story of Arthur's demise, the author of the *Mort* would have surprised contemporary readers with his innovative portrayal of familiar Arthurian figures and his new conception of Arthur's twilight years. Most originally he has combined and modified the existing narratives of Arthur and Lancelot in an attempt to impose closure on their legend:

> et fenist ci son livre si outreement que aprés ce n'en porroit nus riens conter qui n'en mentist de toutes choses. (204:10–13)

Like many a medieval author he has rewritten Arthurian history, yet unashamedly claims historical authenticity and inviolability for his own account.

2. The Tragedy of Arthur's Death: the characters and the plot

Although critics frequently refer to the *Mort* as a tragedy, they generally fail to demonstrate how exactly the work functions as tragic narrative (see *135* for a fuller discussion and bibliography). In the following I shall be using medieval and Aristotelian tragic theory not to imply that the author set out to write a Greek-style tragedy, but to examine the effect the text (its structure and its characters) has on readers. Naturally, the fact that the *Mort* contains two heroes prevents the simplistic application of tragic models. Indeed, our response will depend on whether we read it in isolation or as a branch of the Vulgate Cycle, as the story of Arthur, '*La Mort le Roi Artu*' (1:10), or the story of Lancelot, '*L'Estoire de Lancelot*' (204:9).

Aristotle, in his *Poetics* (*12*), was primarily concerned with describing tragic theatre as a genre, but his assertion that Homeric epic shared many features with Greek tragedy suggests that his comments are applicable also to tragic narrative, i.e. to tragedy as a mode. Of particular relevance to the *Mort* is Aristotle's discussion of:
1. audience response (which he identified as a mixture of fear and pity, leading to catharsis, or a purging of the emotions);
2. the nature of the tragic hero;
3. the relative importance of action and character;
4. the tragic plot, which he described as comprising a *hamartia* (error or false step), *peripeteia* (ironic reversal) and *anagnorisis* (recognition).

For Aristotle, the tragic hero is a man of high social status, so that his fall has far-reaching consequences. He is of intermediate virtue though, for if a morally perfect man met with disaster, the audience would be outraged. If, on the other hand, he were thoroughly evil, his downfall would be merited and the effect would

The Tragedy of Arthur's Death: the characters and the plot

be satisfaction at just deserts. The ironic reversal is triggered by a *hamartia*, an action rather than a character trait, although the false step is related to the hero's personality. The *hamartia* is not, however, a moral defect which would justify what befalls the hero: an ironic chain of events that leads to his downfall. Vital for an audience's tragic response is that the hero's fall be out of all proportion to his initial false step or mistake. Eventually, the protagonist recognises his fate (*anagnorisis*) and sometimes acknowledges his own contribution to it (see *80; 81; 152*).

Aristotle's *Poetics* were unknown to the Middle Ages, yet tragic narratives were produced: they depicted the fall of princes from worldly success into disaster. Sometimes the hero was an innocent victim of misfortune (whose agents could be evil women or envious men), sometimes a proud man whose sin justified his comeuppance (*135*, pp.83-84; *102*, p.2). When, however, such texts presented the hero's punishment as being disproportionate to his fault, the potential for Aristotelian tragic emotion was created.

The *Mort* is an ambiguous narrative, open to various interpretations, as we shall see in Chapter 3. If we decide that human flaws do not justify the downfall of Arthurian civilisation, then our response will be akin to that described by Aristotle. Some critics, however, identify a strong religious ethos running throughout the Vulgate Cycle and argue that the *Mort* functions as a negative *exemplum*, containing characters justly punished for their sins. For those readers the *Mort* is not a tragedy, but a morally improving work like the *Queste*. A further possibility would be to see the *Mort* as advocating *contemptus mundi*, i.e. contempt for the world and all things secular, since it portrays characters whose concern with worldly vanities is shown to be ultimately futile. This interpretation would be equally anti-tragic in the Aristotelian sense.

Even if we decide that the *Mort* depicts man's largely undeserved suffering at the hands of fickle fortune, it cannot be denied that the final paragraphs of the romance seem to mitigate any tragic emotion because of their emphasis on individual salvation. Indeed, if we accept I.A. Richards's view that 'the least touch of any theology which has a compensating Heaven to offer the tragic hero is fatal' (*136*, p.246) then the compensatory salvation won by Lancelot, Gawain and Guinevere must threaten the generation of tragic pathos. Bearing these factors in mind, we shall now consider which of the protagonists in the *Mort* is a/the tragic hero and, by examining possible character flaws, we shall judge the degree to which moral condemnation or fear and pity are the reactions generated by the narrative. A close reading of this final branch of the cycle shows the subtle balance the author achieves between sympathy for the protagonists as frail victims of fortune and of the human condition, and disapproval at their moral failings. In sum, the *Mort* is a medieval Christian tragedy nevertheless rooted in the feudal world. (See Chapter 3 for a detailed analysis of the work's interpretative ambiguities).

The Protagonists

Most tragedies are constructed around one hero, although Aristotle does mention works with a double narrative thread, presenting different outcomes for good and bad characters (*12*, p.49). Several of the *Mort*'s protagonists are treated tragically, almost as if Arthurian society is the collective tragic hero of the work. However, in the branch of the cycle that bears his name, Arthur qualifies best as Aristotelian tragic hero. His status as super-king (for he counts among his vassals seven kings, 107:44–45, and is compared to the biblical King David with his twelve kingdoms, 194:23–25) means that when he falls from a great height, he brings down a whole civilisation. Furthermore, his downfall is precipitated by his best friend Lancelot, his wife, his nephew Gawain, and most poignantly of all, his incestuous son Mordred. Aristotle was right that family relationships make the best tragedy. The flaws most commonly identified in Arthur by modern critics are senility and weakness, the latter already detectable in the later romances of Chrétien (see *141*). While these could produce pity in us, they would not encourage Aristotelian fear, nor the admiration identified in the sixteenth century as a vital ingredient in tragedy (*102*, pp.2–3). The accusations against Arthur of senility (*69*, pp.279–83) and vacillation (*108*) bear some re-examination, however. The fact that Arthur is 92 does

The Tragedy of Arthur's Death: the characters and the plot

not necessarily imply authorial criticism, for in medieval literature advanced age, like that of Charlemagne in French epic and of the patriarchs in the Bible, often commands respect. Besides, many characters, including Guinevere, praise Arthur as 'li plus preudom del monde' (118:8–9). He has also won for himself great loyalty and love over the years and is sincerely mourned by his subjects: 'car c'estoit li princes del monde qui plus estoit amez, car il leur avoit esté touz jorz douz et deboneres' (136:17–19). The narrator admires greatly Arthur's prowess in battle, which is outstanding despite his age, and provides an inspiring example to his men:

> Et celui jor porta li rois Artus armes et le fist si bien qu'il
> n'a el monde home de son aage qui ausi bien le poïst
> avoir fet; encore l'aferme l'estoire qu'il n'i ot de sa
> partie nul chevalier ne viell ne juenne qui si bien le feïst;
> et par essample de son bien fere le firent si bien li suen
> que cil del chastel eüssent esté veincu, se ne fust
> Lancelos. (115:103–10)

This is hardly a man in his dotage; indeed, we must not forget that Gawain is 76, Lancelot 55 (158:60–63) and the queen 50, though still beautiful (4:20–25). In concluding his 'history' of Arthur, the romancer has given his protagonists 'realistically' advanced ages as would befit chronicle tradition; their behaviour, however, recalls the youthful exploits of romance (see *87*).

MacRae is the critic most condemnatory of Arthur's behaviour when he claims that 'Arthur is unwilling or unable to see the situation as it really is and invariably chooses the wrong course of action.' (*108*, p.267). However, in accusing Arthur of weakness and indecisiveness, MacRae fails to take account of the all-pervasive dramatic irony in the *Mort*. Readers are more fully informed of the facts than any of the protagonists, who struggle with incomplete knowledge and conflicting evidence (see *29*). Arthur is not simply unwilling to believe that his wife and Lancelot are committing adultery. He frequently receives information which belies Agravain's accusations, though other indications do support them. By interlacing the different strands of the plot (a technique called *entrelacement*, see Chapter 5) the author has skilfully organised the narrative so as to enhance Arthur's dilemma and thereby win our sympathy for him. When Agravain first accuses Lancelot and the queen of adultery, Arthur is right to disbelieve his nephew since his prior knowledge of them points to their love for and loyalty towards the king (6:21–29; 30:83–89, cf. 30:101–02). Any betrayal is inconceivable, as this would go against their natures. Arthur's only proviso is if Lancelot were a victim of the power of love ('force d'amors', 6:27). Since Arthur has no confirmation of this, rash action at this stage would have been politically disastrous. Nevertheless he plans to 'esprouver la mençonge Agravain' (7:12–13). When a trap to catch the lovers fails, Arthur is pleased not to have acted prematurely (30:46–51), for Lancelot's decision to attend the Winchester tournament while Guinevere stays at court (30:67–70) implies their innocence. His peace of mind is somewhat reinforced by rumours of Lancelot's love for the demoiselle d'Escalot (although Arthur correctly suspects other reasons for Lancelot's absence — an instance of the king's perspicacity) and by reminders of the knight's earlier liaison with the daughter of King Pellés, the mother of Galahad (30:76–83). However, when Arthur is confronted in Morgan's castle with the more concrete pictorial evidence of Lancelot's treachery, he *is* ready to avenge himself:

> 'Je en ferai tant, fet li rois, que se li uns ainme l'autre de fole amor, si com vos me dites, que ge les ferai prendre ensemble ains que cis mois soit passez, se il avient que Lancelos viegne a court dedens celui terme.' (53:77–81, cf. 86:44–47)

Yet, back at Camelot, he discovers that Lancelot has stayed there a mere day and this is clearly odd behaviour from the alleged lover of Guinevere. Consequently, Arthur doubts Morgan's *words* of accusation (62:13), but significantly no reference is made here to the pictures he has *seen*. Is the author hinting that Arthur's response to evidence is partial and biassed? Perhaps, yet the king's prevarication

The Tragedy of Arthur's Death: the characters and the plot 31

is justified, given the undermining of Morgan's evidence by a setting steeped in the *merveilleux* (see *62*). So, can we blame Arthur for not acting at this point? MacRae does, but *he* knows that Lancelot did not love the demoiselle d'Escalot nor Galahad's mother (30:81), and also that the knight's short stay at Camelot resulted from Guinevere's jealous anger. Arthur, however, is not omniscient. He is presented as a victim of circumstances and of that restricted viewpoint characteristic of humankind. Besides, Arthur's reluctance to punish the lovers until concrete proof is forthcoming is a laudable trait, as is his unwillingness to go against the evidence of his heart (see *150*). Indeed, as Gawain and his 'good' brothers later confirm, the disclosure of such a politically sensitive fact would create more problems than refusing to acknowledge the adultery publicly (85:63–84). Eventually Arthur does suspect the lovers, grows angry and even criticises Gawain for his discretion (87:55–59), yet when he attempts to punish Guinevere, the pope, hearing that the lovers had not been caught *in flagrante delicto* (red-handed), forces the king to take her back (117:9–16). Surely the author is not suggesting that the pope is wrong. There is really no satisfactory solution to Arthur's problem; he is in a no-win situation typical of tragedy. In my view, we are being encouraged to sympathise with the king, not criticise him for weakness. Not only do we respect his perspicacity for being the only character to penetrate Lancelot's incognito (§11) and to realise the reasons for his absence, but we also pity him as we are made privy to the anxious thoughts that plague him (7:1–3; 86:41–44). Moreover, since the motives of his advisers are evil (cf. the barons in Beroul's *Tristran*), we approve of his reluctance to act on their accusations: Agravain hates Lancelot (4:14, note the litotes here) and has no real concern for the king's honour (5:1–4), and Morgan 'la desloial' (48:11) is said to hate Lancelot too (54:2–4).

Perhaps there are grounds for criticising Arthur because he listens to malicious information from Mordred and Agravain. Indeed, these evil characters are behind many of the adverse incidents which befall Arthur, as is common in the medieval tragedy of fortune (see *135*, pp.83–84). Agravain (supported by Mordred) forces the adultery into the open (§86) and urges Gaheriet's presence at the ambush in which he is killed (93:65–66). Mordred's treachery is the immediate cause of Arthur's death, facilitated by the king leaving ultimate power in his son's hands. When Arthur gives his kingdom to Mordred, which Guinevere clearly thinks is inadvisable (129:19–23), this could make us question Arthur's judgement. Yet Guinevere's doubts are personal rather than political, and Arthur is unaware of Mordred's desire for the queen. The king is most in error after the entrapment of the lovers and the death of his nephews. While he is surrounded by his immediate family and has the queen at his side he is able to resist the evil characters and to behave as befits a just king. In the later stages of the *Mort*, Arthur falls under the influence of a distraught and vengeful Gawain. Though the king is not presented in a totally negative light, much of the blame for later events being transferred to his nephew, there are signs of royal weakness here and the king must be held ultimately responsible for his decisions.

Scholars also see criticism of Arthur in the Vulgate Cycle's decision to make Mordred his son by incest rather than simply his nephew (see *153*, p.89; *72*; *74*). Mordred is presented throughout the cycle as Gawain's brother and therefore Arthur's sister's son. Their mother (Anna in Geoffrey) is not named in the *Mort*, but she is not Morgan, despite the similarity with Mordred's name. Arthur's paternity is mentioned in the *Lancelot* proper (XCVI, 23–26), but in the same branch Arthur is also called Mordred's uncle (*Lancelot*, LXIX, 1–7). The confusion may be due to the fact that the incest motif was first introduced by the author of the *Mort* and interpolated later into the *Lancelot* (see *69*, pp.31–37; *2*, pp.xvi–xvii; *30*, pp.11–14, 24). Significantly, there is no explicit criticism of Arthur's incest in the *Lancelot*, and in the two passages mentioned above, Mordred alone is blamed for the destruction of Logres. Nor is the incest developed as an ethical issue in the *Mort* (the circumstances of the boy's conception are explained only by later writers, see *30*, pp.14–17) and no moral condemnation of Arthur is expressed by either the protagonists or the narrator. Indeed, the term incest is never used, Mordred being presented simply as Arthur's illegitimate son. It seems likely, therefore, that the incest was introduced by the *Mort* (fairly late, §§135, 141, 164, 190–91) to blacken Mordred's

The Tragedy of Arthur's Death: the characters and the plot

character further and to intensify the Aristotelian-style tragedy of Arthur's death (see *30*, p.24). Mordred's betrayal renders the king victim of a seemingly unavoidable fate, for Arthur realises that his prophetic dream (mentioned in *Lancelot*, XCVI, 24) has been fulfilled: he has unwittingly produced the source of his own destruction:

> 'Ha! Mordret, or me fez tu connoistre que tu ies li serpenz que ge vi jadis eissir de mon ventre, qui ma terre ardoit et se prenoit a moi. Mes onques peres ne fist autretant de fill comme ge ferai de toi, car ge t'ocirrai a mes deus meins...' (164:5–10)

Moreover, the fact that Mordred is Arthur's son intensifies the horror of the treachery, for the marriage he plans with Guinevere (his father's wife) would be an even more heinous form of incest than union with his aunt by marriage (141:31–33). Arthur's incest thus increases the tragic pathos of the *Mort* without stressing his culpability (see *30*, passim; *120*, p.107).

Another character responsible for the final debacle is Gawain, whose obsession with punishing Lancelot for the deaths of his brothers blinds him to the needs of the Arthurian realm. Gawain has been associated with sin ever since Chrétien introduced accusations of murder against him in his *Perceval*, and in the *Queste* it is Gawain who witnesses in a dream the end of the Round Table (*7*, pp.156–57). In the first part of the *Mort*, however, Gawain is presented positively as a noble knight, good adviser to the king and friend to Lancelot. Although he leaps to the wrong conclusion concerning Lancelot and the demoiselle d'Escalot, he sensibly dismisses accusations against the lovers and refuses to attend the burning of the queen (§93). He is also very courteous (his literary reputation as ladies' man is in evidence when he woos the demoiselle d'Escalot) and humbly concedes Lancelot's superiority in the courtship stakes (27:20–40). Later, however, after the death of Gaheriet, he is presented as a ruthless pursuer of revenge, motivated by hatred for Lancelot and his family (115:53–55; 119:125–32; 146:46–55).

Frequently Gawain is shown to be responsible for decisions which go against Arthur's better nature (127:5–28). When Lancelot's female messenger delivers her message, Gawain speaks first, urging the king to avenge his honour and the deaths of his relatives, and reminding him of his oath to destroy the family of King Ban (110:10–22). Arthur's response suggests a certain world-weariness — he feels things have gone too far to turn back, yet realises that Lancelot is 'li hom el monde a qui je devroie plus legierement pardoner un grant meffait, car sans faille il a plus fait pour moi que nus autres chevaliers' (110:25–28). Although Arthur does not forgive Lancelot, the author has clearly set up a tragic conflict in the king's mind between his love for and gratitude towards Lancelot and his concern to protect his honour and please Gawain. During the battle at Joyeuse Garde, Arthur, rescued by Lancelot, recognises the knight's virtue and nobility of heart, and regrets ever having begun the war (116:8–13). However, Gawain's anger at these words indicates that goodwill on the part of Arthur and Lancelot will not suffice to avoid further bloodshed, and soon afterwards we find the king obeying his nephew's wishes, as the phrases 'puis que Gauvains le velt' (119:49–50) and 'puis que vos le voulez' (130:52) indicate.

Several characters recognise that Gawain is to blame for the war between former Knights of the Round Table. Lancelot's messenger stresses the part Gawain will play in his own downfall (110:41–55), and when Lancelot is later informed that Arthur is to pursue him to Gaunes, he identifies the king's nephew as his real enemy (127:16–23, cf. 127:26–28). Gawain's refusal of Lancelot's generous compensation is seen by many as proof that the former is 'orgueillex et oltrecuidiez' (149:10). It seems therefore that at this stage in the narrative Gawain is largely responsible for the imminent destruction of the Arthurian world, Lancelot's magnanimity compensating for any culpability, while Arthur is depicted as torn between loyalty to his family, his kingdom and his former allies. Yet, even at this point Gawain has redeeming features, and never quite forfeits our sympathy. In fact he exhibits many of the heroic features which Aristotle considered necessary to provoke a tragic response. For we are expected to experience not only pity for the hero, but also

The Tragedy of Arthur's Death: the characters and the plot

phobos: that is fear *for* the hero as victim of fate and ultimately mortal, and fear *at* the hero, who represents in his single-mindedness a threat to social stability. Intransigence often characterises the tragic hero and in the *Mort* this quality is most apparent in Gawain. By encouraging a certain stubbornness in Arthur, however, Gawain transfers this tragic trait onto his uncle, the real tragic hero of this branch.

Our sympathy for Gawain (and for Arthur too) is cultivated at the time of his brothers' deaths. The scene in which Arthur and Gawain discover their murdered kin is full of pathos (see Chapter 5). Gawain faints from grief and wishes he were dead himself: 'Ha! Dex, voirement ai ge trop vescu' (101:9–10) he cries, echoing Arthur's words (99:23). Both men realise that whereas lost land can be regained, family can never be replaced (101:10–11; 103:14–21). From this point onwards, uncle and nephew seem to have a death-wish, and when Gawain insists on fighting Lancelot in single combat, Lyonel recognises that the king's nephew, having lost his brothers, cares little whether he lives or dies:

> 'Je vos dirai, fet li rois Lyons, porquoi il le fet en tel maniere; il a si grant duel de ses freres qui sont ocis qu'il voudroit mielz morir que vivre.' (145:59–61)

Gawain confirms this later to Arthur:

> 'et s'il avient qu'il m'ocie, toutevoies sera li deus afinez que ge maing jor et nuit; car sachiez que pour aise estre en aucune maniere, ou morz ou vis, ai je empris ceste bataille.' (146:55–59)

His ruthless pursuit is therefore explained as an extreme reaction to bereavement (see *159*, Chapter V). Gawain is capable of great love, great *sensibilité*, extreme grief and extreme anger. He is also capable of inspiring great affection and loyalty. His squire, who can see that he is pursuing his own destruction, weeps for him, begging him not to proceed, and Arthur is equally upset by the thought that he might lose his remaining nephew (146:35–46) in the combat which he bravely undertakes to end the siege without further bloodshed (§144). During the duel Gawain's reputation is enhanced by the evocation of the solar myth traditionally associated with him and mentioned already in *Lancelot* (LXIX, 2). Significantly, though, the *Mort* attributes the increase of Gawain's strength around midday to the power of baptism (§§153–55). So, when Gawain is at his most vengeful and obstinate, we are nevertheless reminded of his worth and of the tragic loss his death would represent.

When Gawain has been wounded in the head by Lancelot his popularity becomes evident: 'si en pleurent li riche et li povre, car il l'amoient tuit de grant amor' (159:19–20). His heroism is proved by his eagerness to fight the Romans, and as his death approaches we note a growing humility, repentance and acceptance of responsibility for his actions (172:29–32). Pathos and nostalgia are evoked by Gawain's wish to die in his native land of Logres (165:9–11) and to see Lancelot one last time to ask for his forgiveness (165:12–19). Gawain's deathbed advice to Arthur to request Lancelot's help against Mordred is clearly right, but ironically rejected by a king racked by grief and guilt:

'Certes, fait li rois, je me sui tant meffais vers lui que je
ne quit mie que proiere i puist avoir mestier, et por ce ne
l'en requerrai je pas.' (166:28–31)

Arthur repeats this reason when his nephew appears to him in a dream (176:33–35). However, like Gawain, Arthur does not heed warnings, even when he is told that 'ce sera granz domages a toz preudomes' (176:36–37), and they both come to regret it (186:35–46).

Gawain's passing is narrated movingly, his popularity and chivalric excellence demonstrated by the general mourning at his pious death (172:40–43):

et plouroient tout et toutes ausi communement comme
s'il fust cousins germains a chascun; et ce n'estoit mie

> merveille, car mesire Gauvains avoit esté li chevaliers el
> monde plus amés de diverses gens; (173:9–13)

The episode of the Dame de Beloé (§174) provides further proof of his success with the ladies, and his salvation is secured by his generosity to the poor (176:9–15), characteristics already mentioned in the portrait of Gawain in *Lancelot* (LXIX, 2–7). Even after his death, he is remembered affectionately: during the battle of Salisbury King Karados expresses the wish to be buried in Camelot with Gawain (184:66–68) and Arthur regrets his nephew's absence (186:35–46).

Thus Gawain plays a significant role in the destruction of Logres, not least because of his negative influence on the king at a time when Arthur seems ready to respond to the generous, peace-making gestures of Lancelot. However, the author of the *Mort* tempers any negative traits with laudable qualities. Indeed, the king's nephew is shown to be fundamentally a fine, noble knight, who temporarily, while suffering from great grief, behaves in a reckless and selfish way. Although his contribution to the catastrophe is not negligible, it is understandable and we never totally lose sympathy for Arthur's favourite nephew.

While the *Lancelot-Grail* cycle traces the histories of Lancelot, Arthur and the Grail, Lancelot emerges as the hero of the *Prose Lancelot*, although he has to compete with Arthur as the focus of attention in the *Mort*. Lancelot has the social and moral traits required of a tragic hero and he suffers the necessary reversal of fortune. His flaw is, of course, his immoderate love for Guinevere, which various characters foresee will lead to tragic conflict between Lancelot's kin, the descendants of King Ban, and Arthur's family (85:81–84; §87; 89:8–9; 90:87–88). However, as is shown in the *Lancelot* proper, and is corroborated in the *Mort* by the pictures at Morgan's castle (§§51–53) and by the words of Bohort (§59), love is equally the source of Lancelot's superior prowess, which has often benefited Arthur's kingdom. Indeed, Lancelot's final act of beneficial chivalry (inspired posthumously by Guinevere) is his revenge against Mordred's sons for Arthur's death (§197).

Lancelot's fault is to break the rule of courtly discretion, but this is to some extent exonerated by the suggestion that true love is too powerful a force to be resisted (6:26–29). The terms 'espris et alumez' (4:7) imply that Lancelot is the victim of a passion similar to Tristan's for Iseut and recall Ovidian depictions of love characteristic of early medieval romance. Moral criticism is restricted to the paragraphs of the *Mort* which form a bridge with the *Queste*. Yet the *Mort* echoes the more courtly *Lancelot* proper in presenting Guinevere as worthy to inspire love (despite her age). Compare:

> Et la reïne estoit si bele que touz li monz s'en merveilloit, car a celui tens meïsmes qu'ele iert bien en l'aage de cinquante anz estoit si bele dame que en tout le monde ne trouvast l'en mie sa pareille, dont aucun chevalier distrent, por ce que sa biauté ne li failloit nule foiz, que ele estoit fonteinne de toutes biautez. (*Mort*, 4:18–25)

with the narratorial approval expressed in the *Lancelot* when Lancelot first falls for Guinevere:

> Et il n'avoit mie tort, se il ne prisoit envers la roine nule autre dame, car che fu la dame des dames et la fontaine de biauté. (XXIIa, 22).

In the *Mort* Lancelot's choice of a lover is justified by her worth (38:69–76), for she is 'la plus vaillant dame del monde' (119:28). He willingly defends the queen in the *judicium Dei* as a reward for all the goodness she has shown to foreign knights at Arthur's court (74:87–90; 75:36–38). Of course, this is not Lancelot's primary motive, but Gawain confirms his assessment (93:20–22), and so does Arthur, whose love endures despite suspicions of infidelity (79:38–41; 117:17–20). So although the love affair is adulterous and thus reprehensible on the moral and political levels, the superior qualities of Lancelot and Guinevere make it defensible on the courtly and human levels.

The Tragedy of Arthur's Death: the characters and the plot 39

Certainly the queen's jealousy and readiness to doubt Lancelot might suggest that the knight's affections are misplaced (Bohort clearly believes this, §59), yet they could also indicate the intensity of a passion which in despair turns to hatred and revenge (§§32 & 59). During the poisoned fruit episode Guinevere nevertheless remains dignified (§68) and her suffering seems largely unmerited, especially when she is subjected to Bohort's taunts (§77). Later, she genuinely regrets her behaviour towards Lancelot (§§69 & 72), and she places his safety above her own when they are caught together (90:29–35). Thus once the lovers are reconciled, the queen is portrayed positively, as one who deserves the love of both Lancelot and her husband. Indeed, her loyalty to Arthur, whose qualities she praises (139:14), is another commendable feature, as are her strength and resourcefulness (140:1–5) when Mordred tries to force her to marry him (the author here deliberately rewriting the less favourable accounts in Geoffrey (*22*, p. 257), and Wace (*24*, ll.4362–82)). Although Guinevere contributes to Arthur's downfall, it is ironically her excellent qualities — her beauty, generosity and the *bonté* she shows to others (119:26) — which inflame Lancelot's love (and later Mordred's lust), thus triggering the tragic mechanism that leads to everyone's death.

As Adler has suggested, the characters in the *Mort* are Aristotelian in that they are mixed; their negative features do not cancel out their many virtues and their behaviour is often mitigated by the circumstances (*28*, p.937). Our analysis has shown that all the 'good' protagonists have qualities associated with tragic heroes: they are flawed or behave in ways inconsistent with their fundamentally admirable natures. Their downfalls are, however, totally out of proportion to their faults and consequently rich in pathos.

Closely connected to the idea that sin or character flaws are responsible for Arthur's downfall is the view that no one individual is to blame but rather chivalric society itself and the values on which it is built. For Zuurdeeg (*158*), divided loyalties and conflicting ideologies, each represented by different characters, are the cause of the catastrophe. This is partly true. Yet it does not follow that Arthurian values are bankrupt (see Chapter 4) nor are such conflicts unique to Arthur's world. In all societies the potential exists for conflict between two equally admirable ideals or codes of behaviour: love versus duty; family versus friends; honour versus desire. As Vinaver perceptively notes, the tragedy of the *Mort* results from 'the insoluble conflict of "two goods", one symbolized by Lancelot's allegiance to Guinevere, the other by his fidelity to Arthur and Gawain' (*153*, p.89). Other tensions are also present in the work. Arthur has to choose between, on the one hand, his honour, avenging his kin and pleasing his nephew, and, on the other, avoiding a fateful and destructive war against Lancelot (§87). Lancelot has to decide between honouring a promise to the demoiselle d'Escalot or avoiding Guinevere's displeasure. The problem of colliding values and emotions forms an integral part of the tragic plot (see *135*). For in tragedies circumstances are engineered so that the clash of interests and values has far-reaching consequences; because the choices are impossible and made in moments of crisis, they naturally lead to disaster. Such is the role of chance and ill-timed misfortune (*mescheance*) in tragedy.

The Tragic Plot

According to Aristotle, a tragic plot consists of a chain of events set in motion by a false step which eventually leads to the hero's death. Although Arthur is the *tragic* hero of the *Mort* (since Gawain, Lancelot and Guinevere explicitly receive compensatory salvation), it is Lancelot who triggers off the *peripeteia* by making the initial *hamartia*: his promise to the demoiselle d'Escalot to wear her sleeve at a tournament. (Of course, the tragedy was initiated in the *Lancelot* proper by his falling in love with Guinevere). The narrator does not condemn Lancelot when he grants a boon without knowing what the girl will request (the familiar motif of the *don en blanc* which becomes a *don contraignant* (see *113*)); this is a sign of his chivalric generosity and courtesy towards ladies. Moreover, he is especially bound to agree when the girl innocently invokes the thing Lancelot most loves in the world, the queen:

> 'Gentis chevaliers, done moi un don par la foi que tu
> doiz a la riens el monde que tu mieuz ainmes.' (14:2–4)

Thus, ironically, his love for Guinevere results in a promise which places their love in jeopardy. Lancelot realises he is trapped, but cannot escape:

> Quant Lancelos entent ceste requeste, si l'en pesa moult;
> et nequedant il ne li ose contredire, puis qu'il li avoit
> creanté. (14:17–19)

This is a 'no-win' situation typical of tragedy; the very virtues which make Lancelot a great knight and lover (generosity, honour, loyalty, refusal to break his word) also contribute to his downfall. The ironic chain of events set in motion by the rash boon goes as follows: Guinevere learns that her knight has worn another lady's favour at the Winchester tournament. Her jealous anger prolongs their separation, and once reconciled, they become incapable of concealing their passion. This leads to the discovery of the lovers almost *in flagrante delicto* and Lancelot's rescue of the queen from the stake during which Gawain's brothers are accidentally killed. While Arthur, under the influence of Gawain's *desmesure*, pursues Lancelot to Gaunes, treacherous Mordred is left in charge of the kingdom. Even Gawain's convalescence from a wound inflicted by Lancelot is cut short by the untimely arrival of the Roman army. Fighting reopens Gawain's fatal wound, and on the very day Arthur is celebrating victory over the Romans, news of Mordred's treason reaches him. As Arthur's end approaches the pace of the narrative quickens, and he is given no respite from misfortune. The author has created a compressed tragic plot in which timing plays a key role. He does this by modifying his source accounts of the Roman war (see Chapter 1) and by allowing Lancelot to receive news of Guinevere's death on the very day of the battle against Mordred's sons, which will result in Lyonel's demise (§§197–99). Tragic deaths come thick and fast at the end of the *Mort*, none more poignant and futile than when Arthur kills Lucan in a desperate embrace (192:8–24).

Timing clearly plays an important role in the last chapters of the romance and bad luck/misfortune (often blamed by the protagonists for the negative outcome of events, see Chapter 3) are fundamental to the tragic plot throughout. Ironically (and irony is all-pervasive in the *Mort*) coincidence and misunderstandings (the latter often produced unwittingly by Gawain) contribute initially to the stability and well-being of Arthur's court. As long as the king is shielded from the truth by confusing evidence and coincidence, the lovers are protected from his wrath. At the same time though, the rumours and events which protect them also result in their separation, and the consequent intensification of their passion (85:33–39). Arthur's discovery of their infidelity from then on seems inevitable. Nevertheless, the attempted entrapment of the lovers fails, because 'comme aventure estoit' (90:2) Lancelot locks the door when he visits the queen. Luck is on their side, the lovers are not caught red-handed, and this legal nicety is turned to their advantage by the pope's later insistence that Arthur take the queen back (§117). Moreover, the failure to capture them leaves scope for the king to doubt the adultery when Guinevere is returned (118:75–81).

However, the real turning point in the fortunes of the Arthurian world is the killing of Gawain's brothers. The death of Agravain is deliberate and justified, for it seems to come in answer to Lancelot's prayer and he issues a challenge before attacking (94:10–12, 20–27). Similarly Bohort's slaying of Guerrehet is accompanied by a *défi* or challenge, which makes it legally acceptable (94:28–30; see *37*; *121*). Lancelot's killing of Gaheriet, on the other hand, is a mistake, for he did not recognise him (94:54). From then on misfortune prevails, with events conspiring against the protagonists.

As is necessary in tragedy, however, the heroes must seem to be simultaneously victims of adverse circumstances and in control of their fates; if not they would forfeit respectively our sympathy or our interest in the outcome. This tension between an inevitable destiny prophesied long ago and the sense that the actions of the protagonists could still make a difference is created in the *Mort* by the interweaving of terms implying an inexorable chain of misfortune with references to human agency and fault (see Chapter 3). Once

The Tragedy of Arthur's Death: the characters and the plot 43

Gawain's brothers are dead, Arthur and Gawain seem to be the agents of fate, succumbing to a sort of death-wish, and ignoring all warnings of imminent catastrophe. It is Lancelot who attempts to avert disaster through several acts of love and generosity: his rescue of Arthur in battle (§§115–16), his offer of compensation to Gawain rather than fight him in single combat (§147), then his reluctance to kill Gawain when the latter is losing (145:65–72, §157). Lancelot represents the only source of hope in the later stages of the *Mort*, but Arthur refuses to seek his help against Mordred because he feels guilty (176:33–35). Thus Arthur and Gawain's intransigence (perhaps an internal fatality) prevent Lancelot's generosity from saving the Arthurian world. Moreover, Arthur's sense of honour, normally a virtue in Arthurian romance, leads him after Gawain's death to ignore his nephew's warnings and instead to face Mordred alone (176:20–24), placing his trust in God:

> 'Ha! biaus sire Dex Jhesucrist, qui m'avez fet tantes enneurs, puis que ge primes portai coronne et que ge ving a terre tenir, biaus douz sire, par vostre misericorde, ne soufrez que ge perde enneur en ceste bataille, mes donez moi victoire sus mes ennemis qui sont parjuré et desloial envers moi.' (176:40–46)

Yet once Fortune has shown him in a dream the *mescheances* (misfortunes) to come (§§176–77), he evidently believes that he cannot avoid his destiny. Thus, in response to the archbishop's urgent plea to ask Lancelot for help and delay battle with Mordred, the king replies that he is being asked to desist from 'ce dont ge ne me puis retorner' (177:19–20). Repeated reference in §177 to the king's *volenté* implies that if Arthur were to decide otherwise, his kingdom might still be saved. However, Arthur cannot change his mind, for he had earlier sworn to kill Mordred with his own hands (164:9–12) and this has now become a question of honour, reinforced by an oath on his father's soul (177:24–26). Just as earlier, when he swore to Gawain that he would pursue Lancelot to the bitter end and destroy his family's castles (a promise which, the narrator tells us, he will be unable to keep 128:8–15), so now Arthur makes it impossible to turn back without breaking his word.

That Arthur is destined to die during the battle of Salisbury plain is made manifest by the archbishop's interpretation of Merlin's ancient prophecy engraved in a rock:

> EN CESTE PLAINGNE DOIT ESTRE LA BATAILLE MORTEL PAR QUOI LI ROYAUMES DE LOGRES REMEINDRA ORFELINS.(178:19–22)

Even before reading these words, Arthur rides out in full knowledge of his fate: 'comme cil qui bien savoit que en cele plaigne seroit la grant bataille mortex dont Merlins et li autre devineor avoient assez parlé' (178:3–5). Our tragic hero has now reached the point of Aristotelian *anagnorisis* or recognition and is acutely aware of his mortality. While death seems inevitable and Arthur accepts moral responsibility for any adverse outcome, he still places his trust in God and his men:

> 'g'en voi tant que, se ge ne fusse tant venuz avant, je retornasse, quel que talent que ge eüsse eü jusques ci. Mes or soit Jhesucrist en nostre aïde, car ge n'en partirai jamés jusques a tant que Nostre Sires en ait donee enneur a moi ou a Mordret; et se il m'en meschiet, ce sera par mon pechié et par mon outrage, a ce que ge ai greigneur plenté de bons chevaliers que Mordrés n'a.' (178:30–38)

Thus fate and free will, *mescheance* and sin are held in tragic tension right to the end, preventing simplistic moral condemnation of Arthur. This complex narrative elicits fear from us at the self-destructive element in him and pity for his suffering frailty. Indeed, the archbishop's weeping 'tendrement, por ce qu'il ne l'en puet retrere' (178:41–42) functions as a surrogate for the audience's response. The pathos is, however, shattered by the arrival of Mordred's message, offering Arthur the opportunity to withdraw abroad. We are

The Tragedy of Arthur's Death: the characters and the plot 45

thus reminded who the real villain is, and approve Arthur's promise to kill him with his own hands (179:7, cf. 164:9–12).

Arthur confronts his destiny with great dignity (see *68*), refusing to abandon the code of honour for which he was renowned and insisting even during the course of the battle that *either* himself *or* Mordred will die :'veu ge a Dieu qu'il couvient ici morir moi ou Mordret' (190:48–49) — thus contradicting the prophecies which warn of total destruction. In this way he asserts his free will, despite the fact that the outcome of events has long been known and foreseen. So he functions like a tragic hero, whose inevitable, imminent death forces us to confront our own mortality. This realisation of the fate common to all mankind adds an important aspect to Aristotle's concept of *anagnorisis*. The final paragraphs of the *Mort* not only arouse admiration for the chivalry, prowess and *sensibilité* of Arthur and his great knights and pity for their suffering, but also remind us of the frailty of the greatest men.

As we shall see in Chapter 3 the *Mort* adopts a secular view of history, which concentrates on the world of the flesh with death (rather than salvation) as its final phase. The viewpoint is man's: limited and imperfect, not God's, hence few answers are provided to the protagonists' existential questions. In creating mitigating circumstances for the behaviour of his flawed characters, the author is encouraging us to view these Arthurian figures as tragic heroes, victims of fate, fortune and bad timing. However, at the very end of the work, in what Lyons (*107*) perceptively calls the epilogue, the worldly perspective is replaced by a more Christian, spiritual one when we are assured of the salvation of Lancelot (202:26–30), Guinevere (197:15–17, where her repentance is stressed) and Gawain (§176). For some readers, this would be enough to destroy the tragic effect. However, even the saved, Lancelot, Gawain and Guinevere, suffer enough to merit our pity. Yet the truly tragic hero is Arthur, whose final act (for which he blames Fortune) is to kill Lucan in a desperate, but well-intentioned embrace (192:8–24). Imprecise references to a Christian burial are no assurance of his salvation, and nor is there any compensation offered to the civilisation which bore his name. For at the battle of Salisbury the flower of Arthurian chivalry is wiped out:

> Einsi commença la bataille ... dont li roiaumes de Logres fu tornez a destrucion, et ausi furent meint autre, car puis n'i ot autant de preudomes comme il i avoit eü devant; si en remestrent aprés leur mort les terres gastes et essilliees, et soufreteuses de bons seigneurs, car il furent trestout ocis a grant douleur et a grant haschiee. (181:51–58)

This emphasis on loss, destruction and irreplaceability, the general lamenting and consequent pathos, and the predominantly secular ethos of the whole work prevent the tragic emotion generated earlier from being totally dissipated by a few paragraphs devoted to individual salvation at the end.

The final branch of the Vulgate Cycle is a Christian tragedy, which primarily stresses the suffering of its protagonists in *this* world. It is not a fate-tragedy, nor is it a tragedy of the proud man or an *exemplum* on the *contemptus mundi* theme. The *Mort* is probably the first example of that distinctively medieval hybrid, the romance tragedy (see 59, p.213), which combined a love story with the fall of a prince. Although ignorant of the theory of Aristotle, the author has produced a work containing nuanced characters whose behaviour resists facile moral judgement. The humanity with which difficult issues are treated and the inexorability of the tragic plot tend to generate sympathy in the audience. However, the *Mort* also raises questions concerning the interpretation of events in human lives, the meaning of secular history, and this will be the subject of Chapter 3.

3. Interpreting Arthurian History: the quest for meaning

In the same way that our sensitivity to tragic narrative depends on our world-view, so medieval readers would have responded to the *Mort* according to the model of history they espoused. In this chapter we shall analyse the cyclic romance against a background of medieval historiography and consider how far the pseudo-historicity of Arthur affected the interpretation of events narrated in the *Mort*. The characters' own attempts at explanation and the narrator's commentary will be investigated in order to identify the possible audience responses provoked by the narrative.

The 'historical' approach is justified because whereas the figure of Lancelot was the product of the French literary imagination, conceived within the genre of romance, King Arthur was presented by some Anglo-Norman chroniclers as a historical character, whose reign really had marked a highpoint in the British past (see *76*; *77*; *127*). The French author of the *Mort*, influenced by Tristan romances, continued the story of Lancelot and Guinevere by presenting open conflict between the lovers and society. Yet he also linked it with a narrative on Arthur's demise supplied by the pseudo-histories of Geoffrey and Wace, thus producing a hybrid work which combined features of medieval romance and historiography.

The author of the *Mort* rewrites Arthurian romance tradition, yet also imitates medieval historians in presenting his work as authentic and true (204:10–13). Most writers treating of Arthur were keen to have their narratives designated as *historiae* rather than *fabulae* (accounts of unnatural events which neither did nor could have occurred) and the author of the *Mort* was no exception. The first history to mention Arthur and his battles was the *Historia Brittonum* (9thC) attributed to Nennius, but Geoffrey of Monmouth's *Historia* was the first historiographical treatment of the Arthurian legend. Although Geoffrey did not convince all of his contemporaries, for some, like William of Newburgh and Gerald of Wales, accused him of lying (see *142*, pp.5–6), he presents his work as a true account of British history, written in Latin prose (the authoritative medium) and based on a very ancient book in the British tongue, which Geoffrey claimed belonged to a certain Walter, Archdeacon of Oxford (*22*, p.51). The use of prose and the ascription of branches of the Vulgate Cycle to Walter Map may be an attempt to give the cyclic romance historical credentials, the false attribution perhaps also arising from a conflation of two learned archdeacons of Oxford, both called Walter.

Wace's *Brut* was written in the vernacular in octosyllabic verse (the usual metre of twelfth-century romance *and* historiography). It was commended to its public as a true record and a translation of an authoritative Latin source (see *84*). In contrast, Chrétien made little pretence of historical veracity in his romances, though he did claim written sources for his *Cligés* and his *Perceval*. His treatment of Arthurian material is ahistorical and his romances lack spatio-temporal precision. Yet in manuscript fonds français 1450 in the Bibliothèque Nationale de France a scribe has inserted Chrétien's five romances into the *Brut* at the point (ll.1057–70) where Wace mentions a long period of peace in Arthur's reign, during which, he suggests, the adventures narrated by storytellers must have occurred. While Wace rejects the truthfulness of these stories on the grounds of rhetorical overembellishment, the thirteenth-century scribe/compiler of BNF f.fr. 1450, in incorporating Chrétien's romances into the *Brut*, treats them as Arthurian history. A parallel shift from romance to history is to be found in the Vulgate Cycle; for the *Lancelot* proper places material from Chrétien's ahistorical romance, the *Charrete*, into the pseudo-historical context of Arthur's war with Ban, which is then combined with pseudo-Salvation History in the *Queste* (and later in the *Estoire*, *Merlin* and *Suite*), the final branch returning to more secular history with Arthur's death. Throughout the *Lancelot-Grail* cycle, composed in the prose favoured by 13th-century history writing, the subjective intrusions of a narrator are kept to the minimum (see *56*). The story, *li contes*, achieves an autonomy and objectivity of its own, deriving its authority from the eyewitness accounts supplied by Arthur's knights, recorded by his clerks and translated/set down by 'Gautier Map' (see *Queste*, pp.279–80; *Mort*, §204).

The *Mort* creates the fiction of historicity by invoking an authoritative author, Walter Map, who set down in writing the adventures of Arthur and the Grail at the instigation of another historical figure, Henry II of England, a king who during his lifetime encouraged comparison between himself and the illustrious King Arthur (see *32*). Although no source is mentioned, the term 'mis en escrit' (1:1–2) suggests translation (indeed in some manuscript copies we find 'translaté'). The implication is that as with the *Aventures del Seint Graal* (dictated by Bohort and written down (in Latin?) by Arthur's clerks, 2:9–12) the *Mort* is based on an eyewitness account written down in authoritative Latin. Although the narrative is frequently designated a *conte* (52 occurrences, see *6*, pp.313–14), it is on six occasions called an *estoire*, with its connotations of a history authorised by a reliable source: 57:41; 115:106; 129:35; 175:23; 190:56; 204:9 (*6*, pp.533–34), the last referring to the romance as *L'Estoire de Lancelot*.

Since the events of history are known and unchangeable, the author does not seek to create suspense. His role is to commemorate, to tell *how* the knights of the Round Table met their ends, *how* Arthur was mortally wounded during the battle of Salisbury and *how* no-one had seen him since, hence the repetition in the prologue of the terms *conment* and verbs related to memory: *ramentevoit/ ameneües* (§1). However, medieval historiography was also interested in the relevance of the past to the present and questioned *why* events occurred, and whether any lessons could be learned from them. Several explanations for the rise and fall of secular empires existed in the Middle Ages and what concerns us here is to discover which model(s) the author of the *Mort* may be using when suggesting an interpretation of the 'historical' *données* he inherited.

Medieval Historiography: Augustine or Boethius?

According to F.P. Pickering medieval writers wishing to depict events in this world had a choice between two historiographical models: 'after Augustine' and 'after Boethius' (*132*, cf. *135*). The writings of St. Augustine of Hippo (4th–5thC) were concerned with Salvation History and placed all human affairs within the framework of two cities (the earthly and the heavenly) and 6 ages of man. After the six historical ages, Augustine added two eschatological ages (based on the teaching of the last things as found in the Apocalypse): the Last Judgement and the resurrection of the righteous. He saw world events as part of God's plan, in which there was no role for chance or fickle fortune. According to the Augustinian scheme, people in the Middle Ages found themselves in the sixth age equated with human senility. They were waiting for the second coming of Christ and hoping to be accepted into the heavenly Jerusalem. Indeed, followers of Joachim de Fiore, whose teaching was influential in the thirteenth century (see *100*) felt that the apocalyptic finale to world history was nigh and looked for signs of the coming of Christ and Antichrist in everyday events.

Boethius's *Consolation of Philosophy* (6thC, *14*), however, provided medieval man with a different way of interpreting secular history. This influential first-person narrative presents the reflections of a prisoner awaiting death and his conversations with Philosophy, who appears to him in prison to console him. Although the narrator begins by criticising fickle Fortune for his undeserved downfall, Philosophy eventually teaches him that Fortune is God's handmaiden, fulfilling the divine will. The message of the *Consolation* is ultimately stoic; man must not place all his trust in the vanities of life and the favours of fortune. Although Boethius mentions God, Divine Providence, Fate and Fortune, there is no reference to Christ or to salvation. Thus, in dealing exclusively with man's lot in this world and the transience of earthly existence, he offers a convenient model for the treatment of dynastic, secular history.

Fundamentally, Augustine and Boethius had more in common than Pickering's opposition suggests, for both authors agreed that Divine Providence operates in the world and that man blames fickle Fortune for his adversity simply because he is incapable of understanding God's overall plan. However, many medieval writers read the hugely popular *Consolation* selectively, preferring the

Interpreting Arthurian History: the quest for meaning

presentation of amoral Fortune in Books I and II, before Philosophy has convinced the prisoner of her moral function. So, in the following textual analysis the term Augustinian will be used for the providential model of history, while the term Boethian will designate the view of history presented in the *Consolation*, Books I and II, which depict a Fortune who sends success or adversity to man irrespective of merit. This concept is symbolised by the popular image in medieval iconography of the blindfolded goddess turning her wheel capriciously, and toppling the fortunate from the pinnacle of their success. The presence of amoral fortune, which explains the sudden and unmerited reversals of man's existence, creates the potential for tragedy in the *Mort*, despite the co-existence of Augustinian elements.

Prior to the thirteenth century and following Augustine, Christian historiographers came to view the rise and fall of empires and the transference of power from one race to another as implementing God's design to Christianise the world; the triumphs and failures of the past providing positive and negative *exempla* to instruct medieval man (see 76). Similarly, Anglo-Norman historians after the conquest justified their political success in terms of God's punishment of a sinful people (the Saxons). They modified, however, the providential view of history, giving a greater role to purely human causation and to Fortune, and emphasising the cyclical nature of history. In Geoffrey's *Historia* human sin is often portrayed as the cause of dynastic catastrophes, although in the Arthurian section the role of Boethian Fortune in bringing down great men counterbalances hints at human folly (see 71).

Wace's *Brut* is even less providentialist than its source and fortune is not implicated in Arthur's downfall. Yet the *Brut* poses questions concerning how to read the lessons of history (see 84) and the Norman poet (like the Vulgate authors) is interested in the clerk's role in commemorating the past. Wace emphasises the exemplary chivalry and *courtoisie* of Arthur's reign, but his narrator (the voice he creates to comment on the action) is reticent when it comes to explaining his downfall. Arthur is simply the victim of treachery. Likewise, the author of the *Didot Perceval* introduces little commentary into his work, though he does suggest that Arthur's triumphs (against the Romans and against the Saxon pagans who aid Mordred) are granted by God. On the other hand, the disasters — the deaths of Gawain and King Lot — are the result of *mescaance* (*20*, ll.2578, 2598) and when Arthur is mortally wounded in the battle in which 'molt i ot mors de buens cevaliers' (*20*, ll.2639–40), there is no suggestion that this is a punishment for sin.

The author of the *Mort* was probably influenced by the interpretations of British history offered by his predecessors. However, some critics argue that a more influential interpretative framework was provided by Grail history as presented in the *Queste*. The idea, introduced by Robert de Boron, that Britain was Christianised through the arrival during Arthur's life of the holy and sacramental Grail enabled future authors to view Arthurian legend as part of the history of Christianity and to interpret its successes and failures in providential terms. Moreover, the emphasis on genealogy (the notion of a lineage of grailkeepers and grailwinners) and the use of prefiguration and the fulfilment of prophecy as devices linking the different branches of the Vulgate Cycle indicate that the Arthurian era had been integrated (albeit analogically) into Salvation History. Thus Galahad's arrival at court in the *Queste* would correspond to Christ's second coming, and the destruction of the Arthurian world once the adventures of the holy Grail had been completed would constitute a sort of apocalypse. Indeed, Micha (*117*, p.162) sees the *Prose Lancelot* in just such terms — the 'Old Testament' *Lancelot* proper prefiguring the revelation of the truth in the 'New Testament' *Queste* and the latter prophesying the apocalyptic finale found in the *Mort*.

In broad terms this interpretation of the *Mort* is valid, though very different from the attitude towards Arthurian history exhibited by its more Boethian sources, Geoffrey and Wace. A closer analysis of the *Mort* demonstrates, however, that its answer to the question why the kingdom falls is certainly not as clear-cut as that of the *Queste*, which, in Gawain's premonitory dream, blames human pride and lust for the demise of the Round Table (pp.155–57). Whereas the *Queste*'s hermits identify for the benefit of both questers and readers unequivocal Christian meanings in the Grail adventures, there are no such omniscient figures in the *Mort*. Nor is there much narratorial commentary aimed at manipulating our reaction and we therefore have to work much harder at understanding the final branch of the cycle.

Interpreting the 'Mort Artu'

Despite a lack of narratorial commentary the author is nevertheless interested in the problems of interpretation which readers, both medieval and modern, share with the Arthurian characters. This interest is revealed in two ways. Throughout the *Mort* there are letters, paintings, epitaphs, inscriptions, oaths and prophecies, evidence of various kinds which requires interpreting, and from which it is always possible to draw false conclusions (see *60*; *144*). Secondly, the protagonists are shown constantly questioning the reasons behind the events which befall them and struggling to ascertain the truth in a world full of deception, misunderstanding and ambiguous signs (see *29*). Their interrogatory stance and desire to arrive logically at the truth are reflected in the language they use, which abounds in hypothetical conditions. Arthur frequently expresses himself in this way when attempting to interpret evidence concerning the affair between Lancelot and Guinevere. However, conflicting information and fragmentary knowledge prevent him from arriving easily at the truth, as we saw in Chapter 2. Gawain, too, is unable for a long time to work out who the unknown knight at the Winchester tournament is, despite his enquiries, and when he does realise, draws false conclusions concerning the champion's relationship with the demoiselle d'Escalot. The queen, who thought that Lancelot was the most loyal lover in the world, is thrown into turmoil by Gawain's erroneous claims, and when she banishes Lancelot from her presence, he is equally confused. When misfortune befalls characters they do not know whom to blame — are they being punished for some sin or are they the hapless victims of bad luck? Such questions are posed by Guinevere during the poisoned fruit episode (62:82–84), by Arthur and Gawain on the deaths of their relatives (§§99–103), and by many Arthurian knights as they witness the destruction of Logres.

This need to identify the final cause lurking behind the efficient cause (the latter explaining *how* a particular effect is created, the former explaining *why*) is especially evident in modern criticism on the *Mort*. Encouraged by the *Queste* author's moralising to expect worldly success to reward virtue and failure to result from sin or fault, scholars look for moral reasons to explain Arthur's downfall. Although they acknowledge the importance of fate and fortune in the *Mort*, modern readers tend to emphasize faults either in the main characters or deep within Arthurian society, its values and institutions as the causes of the catastrophe (see *40; 69; 108; 158*). It is generally assumed that Arthur's world, flawed, decadent or too secular, deserves to collapse (see Chapter 4). An exception to this trend though is Faith Lyons, who stresses the positive qualities of Arthurian civilisation and places a more Boethian interpretation on events when she concludes that 'ill-timed misfortune and tragic accident' are the primary causes of its demise (*107*, p.147).

The moral flaws which the prose romancer may be suggesting brought about the end of Arthurian civilisation are the following: Arthur's act of incest which produced Mordred, his weakness and senility, and his obstinacy in pursuit of Lancelot; the adultery of Lancelot and Guinevere (a sin against the sacrament of marriage and the bonds of friendship and allegiance); the queen's jealousy; the *desmesure* of Gawain; the evil motives of Mordred, Agravain and Morgan, who pursue their own selfish ends. These flaws were discussed in Chapter 2. What concerns us here are the explanations — ethical or otherwise — provided by narrator or characters when things go wrong. What one finds are two sets of conflicting terms interwoven throughout the *Mort*. On the one hand, there are references to coincidence, bad luck and the amoral behaviour of Fortune, the key words here being *aventure*, *mesaventure* and *mescheance* (see *93; 94; 135*). The characters thus seem to be the victims of fortuitous circumstances beyond their control. On the other hand, appeals to a God, who is thought to intervene personally in human affairs, references to sin and to vices such as *orgueil* and

Interpreting Arthurian History: the quest for meaning

outrage, and admissions of guilt all give the impression that the characters are morally responsible for their actions and that disaster may represent divine punishment.

The interweaving and juxtaposition of these different explanations produces ambiguity, heightened by our uncertainty as to whether the author shares the opinions expressed by his fictional characters or whether he is distancing himself ironically from them. The reader's situation is further complicated by the difficulty of interpreting ambiguous terms like *pechié* and *mescheance*. The primary meaning of *pechié* is sin, but its secondary meaning is misfortune, whereas *mescheance* usually means bad luck, misfortune or just failure, but can sometimes imply moral guilt. Furthermore, the ubiquitous phrase 'il avint que', although formulaic, nevertheless suggests that characters are victims of a series of unfortunate coincidences that befall them. However, it also shares some of the connotations which the term *aventure* has in medieval romance; for although events appear to be chance happenings, the frequency with which the characters are plagued by unlucky coincidences may point to an overall design at work. One is then left wondering if this overall design should be equated with Divine Providence (as it is in the *Queste*) or with a more pagan notion of fate or destiny. The following analysis is intended to demonstrate the subtlety with which the author of the *Mort* raises the issue of *why* Arthur's world collapses without imposing on the reader an unequivocal answer to this question.

Sin and Misadventure

Ambiguity is present at the very beginning of the *Mort* when Gawain, having failed miserably to discover the secrets of the Grail, admits to having killed eighteen of his fellow knights on the quest 'par mon pechié' (3:24), but also because 'la mescheance se torna plus vers moi que vers nul de mes compaignons' (3:21–23). Gawain seems to be implying that his victory over (and killing of) other knights was not so much the result of his superior chivalric competence, but because he was unlucky. *Mescheance* is mentioned twice (3:17, 21), on both occasions with the meaning 'misfortune', and given the parallelism of the two sentences in lines 18–25 (both times denying that *chevalerie* was the cause of the killing), it seems likely that *pechié* in line 24 means 'bad luck' too. Arthur's reply is equally equivocal, 'voirement a ce esté mescheance droite, et je sei bien que ce vos est avenu par vostre pechié' (3:26–27). He may also be using the term *pechié* (3:27) in its secondary meaning, having agreed with his nephew that this killing was indeed *mescheance droite*. Although this is the interpretation I favour for this exchange, there is no denying the possibility of a more censorious reading here and the (probably deliberate) element of ambiguity. The *Mort* thus begins on a note of failure, murder and possibly sin, though misfortune seems to have played its part too. This atmosphere is further intensified by the narrator's reference to Lancelot falling back into the sin of adultery with Guinevere, 'si qu'il rencheï el pechié de la reïne' (4:8–9). However, these words were written to form a link with the *Queste* (of the seven references to *pechié* in the whole of the *Mort*, four occur in paragraphs 3 and 4, see *6*), and lose much of their moral force when the author stresses the courtly consequences of indiscretion, rather than the spiritual ones. Nowhere else is their love referred to as *pechié* and when the term *fole* is attached to it this is mostly by people maliciously accusing the lovers of 'fole amour' (*6*, pp.74–76). The author's conception of love (see Chapter 4) seems to imply a loss of free will on the part of lovers, thus mitigating their guilt. The coercive nature of love is recognised by Arthur (6:27–29) and by the demoiselle d'Escalot, who cannot escape her passion for Lancelot (which she refers to as *mescheance*, 57:31) and is therefore destined to die for him: 'car il m'est ensi destiné que je muire por lui' (39:19–20). Bohort regrets the day Lancelot ever fell in love with Guinevere, seeing their love as the result of Fortune's (or misfortune's) intervention: 'ne Fortune n'assembla onques l'amor de vos deus en tel maniere come ge la vi assemblee fors por nostre grant domage' (59:15–17). His view of love is negative, yet still casts the lovers in the role of victims. However, Bohort's opinion is counterbalanced by Lancelot's courtly conception of his relationship with Guinevere. His love is unavoidable, yet he loves willingly (note the repetition of the term *volenté*, §38), his passion justified by Guinevere's excellent qualities and the chivalric perfection she

Interpreting Arthurian History: the quest for meaning

inspires in him. Thus illicit love, seen by some as the root cause of Arthur's downfall (see 2, p.x), is both condemned and defended by the protagonists, while the author's ethical standpoint remains unclear. Indeed, the fact that the lovers avoid the violent deaths of other Arthurian figures and win salvation suggests that their culpability is minimal (see 29). In this respect the *Mort* shares the ethos of the *Lancelot* proper.

Lancelot's woundings early in the work have been interpreted as divine warnings or punishments for his return to the secular life, with its sexual love and tournaments, which the *Queste* condemned (see 69, p.232; 89). Yet Lancelot's accidental wounding in the forest is introduced by the phrase 'si avint que' (64:27; cf. 64:35), Lancelot attributes the huntsman's arrival there to *male aventure* (64:45–46) and his doctor calls the event *droite mescheance* (65:27), all suggesting that this is an unlucky incident rather than a divine sign. The possibility remains, nevertheless, that the author is agreeing with Boethius's character Philosophy in conceiving of Fortune as the handmaiden of God.

God plays a minor role in the early part of the story. Lancelot and his doctors claim that wounds can be healed only with God's help (41:6, 24, 53–61) and He is expected to distinguish right from might in the *judicium Dei* (68:25; 84:12–17; 144:73; 146:52; 148:29). Occasionally, misfortune is linked with the withdrawal of divine protection. Lancelot assures Bohort that 'cil qui jusques ci m'a soufert a avoir victoire en touz les leus ou ge ai esté ne souferra pas par sa grace que il me meschiee en leu ou ge soie' (60:81–84) and Guinevere, accusing God of abandoning her when she kills Mador's brother by mistake, 'dit que bien l'a Dex oubliee quant par tel mescheance a ocis un si preudome' (62:82–83). It has been suggested that the poisoned fruit episode which threatens Guinevere's life is just punishment for the queen's treatment of her faithful lover and for her Eve-like role throughout the Vulgate Cycle. Yet apart from the obvious biblical connotations of the fruit (never called an apple though) and Bohort's list of women who, according to tradition, brought down famous men (§59), there is little textual evidence to support the view that Guinevere is a sinful woman receiving her just deserts. Most commentators on the killing of Gaheris (including the narrator) speak of *(mes)aventure* or *mescheance* (62:37, 44, 53, 78; 63:2; 77:28, see *6*) rather than guilt, and the queen is exonerated by the judicial combat. A similar *aventure* which has little to do with God's workings is Arthur's arrival at Morgan's castle, an episode which contains most of the fairy magic in the *Mort* (see *123*). 'Morgan la desloial' is associated with the Celtic *merveilleux*, reflected in the terms employed in this episode (48:76, 82; 49:14). Although Arthur thinks that God has given him the opportunity to see his sister again (50:61–64), the narrator, through the ironic use of 'il avint que' (51:7), hints at Morgan's machinations, and that a more malign force is behind the revelation of the queen's infidelity as depicted in the painted room. This is neither bad luck nor God's will, but the influence of evil, whose instruments in this text are Mordred, Morgan and Agravain.

Whereas characters (like Boethius's prisoner) are on the whole reluctant to impute their misfortune to God, unless they are willing to accept some moral responsibility for it, they are keen to attribute their good luck to divine aid. Lancelot feels that God enabled him to escape when caught almost red-handed with the queen (90:84), perhaps in response to the lovers' earlier invocation of divine help (90:29–35, 61). It is unclear whether or not the narrator shares this view (unlike Beroul's intrusive narrator in his *Tristran*, 1.960), though we are told that Lancelot locked the door to the queen's chamber 'si comme aventure estoit qu'il n'i devoit pas estre ocis' (90:2–3). Is this simply a statement by the omniscient narrator that as luck would have it Lancelot was not killed that day, or does the verb *devoit* imply that he is being protected? The narrator is slightly less non-committal later, when Guinevere is rescued from the pyre and replies to Lancelot 'comme cele qui estoit liee de ceste aventure que Dex li avoit envoiee' (95:9–11). Conceivably, though, the narrator is here expressing the queen's opinion.

There is some evidence that God or good luck (perhaps pagan Fortune) is protecting the lovers in the first part of the *Mort*, for despite their suffering, their liaison is for a while concealed by their prolonged separations. However, the height of misfortune is reached

Interpreting Arthurian History: the quest for meaning

when Arthur's nephews are killed during the rescue of Guinevere. This event, even more than the adultery, precipitates Arthurian society towards the abyss. While Lancelot's killing of Agravain could be interpreted as God's answer to Lancelot's prayer (94:10–12) and as just revenge on this evil brother for his conniving against the lovers (cf. Tristan's punishment of the barons), there is no moral justification for the death of Gaheriet. Significantly, Gaheriet does not wish to fight Lancelot; it is Agravain who forces him to be present (93:65–66) and Gaheriet's death is thus brought about by one of the ill-intentioned characters. Besides, it seems that fate has now taken over and that the time has come for Gaheriet to die. Whereas Arthur had earlier managed to avoid conflict between Lancelot and his nephews by refusing to allow Gawain and Gaheriet to take part in the Winchester tournament (16:70–76), he is here unable to resist the pressure from Agravain, and Gaheriet is forced to join in the fateful and fatal attack.

It is unlikely though that Agravain represents an instrument of divine justice. Arthur explicitly rejects this notion, for although his lament seems to make a connection between God's favours and good fortune:

> 'Ha! Dex, tant m'avez meintenu en grant enneur, et or sui en pou d'eure abessiez par droite mescheance, que nus hom ne perdi tant comme j'ai perdu.' (103:10–13)

he concludes that *mescheance* and Lancelot's pride are to blame:

> 'Ceste perte ne m'est pas avenue par la justise Damledieu, mes par l'orgueill Lancelot.' (103:21–23)

Gawain blames only Fortune at this stage:

> 'Biaus douz frere, comment pot soufrir Fortune vostre destruiement si let et si vilain, qui vos avoit garni de toutes bontez?' (100:52–54)

Having presented various different interpretations of the event, the narrator leaves us to decide whether to agree with the protagonists or to be sceptical of their opinions.

From this point onwards, references to moral responsibility and guilt are mostly attached to Gawain and Arthur as they pursue Lancelot relentlessly. King Yon tries to dissuade them from this course of action, suggesting that a war against the descendants of King Ban would go against the will of God and therefore result in disaster: 'car nos apertement savons que Nostres Sires l'a eslevé par desus touz autres lingnajes' (104:11–13). This is the only explicitly 'Augustinian' statement in the *Mort*, with its suggestion that a particular family (that of Lancelot and his son Galahad) has a special God-given mission. Yon's warning, however, goes unheeded, for Arthur and his knights are more concerned with honour and revenge than with the need to preserve the peace or to consider God's will (104:56–71).

The behaviour of Arthur and Gawain is clearly reprehensible here, especially in comparison with the magnanimity of Lancelot, yet the narrator rarely apportions blame. Moral ambiguity is maintained by a liberal sprinkling of allusions to Fortune and *mescheance*, though the latter sometimes simply means failure, especially in battle (see 6). Furthermore, our sympathy for the king and his nephew is encouraged through emphasis on their grief, suffering and redeeming features (see Chapter 2).

In the later stages of the *Mort* our interpretation of events is complicated by several predictions made by the characters and the narrator. Arthur's decision to attack Lancelot at Joyeuse Garde is accompanied by the following narratorial comment:

> Einsint fu la guerre emprise qui puis torna au domage le
> roi Artu; et comment qu'il fussent au commencement au
> desus, il furent desconfit en la fin. (105:11–14)

and when Mordred is left in charge of Logres, and Arthur encourages his vassals to swear allegiance to his nephew/son, the narrator says ominously:

> et cil firent le serement dont li rois se repenti puis si
> douleureusement qu'il en dut estre vaincuz en champ en la
> plaigne de Salesbieres ou la bataille mortex fu, si come
> ceste estoire meïsmes le devisera apertement. (129:31–
> 36)

These comments may be designed to imply criticism of Arthur's behaviour, the narrator emphasising the negative consequences of his actions, but they also enhance his status as tragic victim of an inescapable fate.

The atmosphere of doom is intensified when Lancelot's female messenger to Arthur's camp warns the king of his imminent death, which seems already to have been foretold by 'li sage home' (110:40–41), and reminds Gawain of his ominous vision at the Grail Castle (cf. *Lancelot*, LXVI, 19–21). Like Gawain, we know from the hermit's interpretation of the dream depicting a serpent fighting a leopard (*Lancelot*, LXVI, 37–38) that Arthur will be incapable of winning the war fought abroad against an unknown knight, that Gawain will die, Arthur's subjects will betray him and all will be killed in civil strife. Although such a prophecy might imply that this manner of death is inevitable, the damsel also stresses the characters' responsibility for their fates, suggesting that their destinies are not unavoidable:

> 'Et vos, messire Gauvain ... estes li plus fox de touz les
> autres, et assez plus que ge ne cuidoie; car vos
> pourchaciez vostre mort, et si le poez veoir tout
> apertement ... S'il vos souvenist bien des merveilles [of
> the prophetic vision] ... et de la senefiance que li
> hermites vos devisa, ja ceste guerre ne fust, tant com vos
> la poïssiez destorner. Mes vostre maus cuers et vostre
> granz mescheance vos chace en ceste emprise.' (110:41–
> 54)

Mescheance in line 53 probably means sin, especially when juxtaposed with *maus cuers*, yet some ambiguity remains. The general tenor of the girl's speech is echoed by the old lady in §131, where Arthur is castigated for following Gawain's *fol conseil*.

This raises the question of how to interpret the numerous prophetic remarks, dreams and visions (some of which link up with earlier parts of the cycle) and in particular Merlin's prophecy carved in the rock on Salisbury Plain (§178, see *110*, pp.58–63). Do they imply that man is ultimately incapable of changing his destiny or are they warnings which characters refuse to heed and which thus underline their *desmesure* and blind obstinacy? Does Merlin, like God, foresee events without denying man his free will to act but then accept the consequences? The author does not offer solutions to these difficult philosophical questions. Indeed, even the hermit in the *Queste*, who interprets Gawain's prophetic dream, is rather vague and ambiguous regarding the knight's ability to prevent the destruction of Arthurian civilisation (represented in the last part of the allegorical dream):

> 'La darreaine parole de vostre songe, fet il [the hermit], ne vos dirai je pas, car ce seroit une chose dont ja preu ne vendroit, et si vos en porroit len mauvesement destorner.' (*Queste*, p.157)

Whatever the significance of the prophecies in the *Mort*, one of their effects is undoubtedly to increase the tragic pathos.

The theme of moral responsibility is more frequently mentioned by the protagonists as they approach the dénouement. Arthur blames Lancelot's *orgueill* (103:22) for beginning the war, then Gawain (144:7–13) for forcing him to prosecute it and finally Gawain's *outrage* (159:11–12) and his *felonnie* (165:22) for the catastrophic conclusion. However, Arthur's castigation of his nephew is softened by his praise of Gawain's chivalry and by the grief and pathos with which he chides the knight for bringing about his own downfall. Despite Gawain's instruction (a form of *anagnorisis*) to give his own *outrage* as the cause of his death on his epitaph (172:30), Arthur cannot accept that his nephew's passing is in any

Interpreting Arthurian History: the quest for meaning 63

way justified. His lament accuses fickle Fortune and her ally, death, neither of whom seems to operate according to any sense of justice:

> 'Hé! Fortune, chose contrere et diverse, la plus desloial chose qui soit el monde, por quoi me fus tu onques si debonere ne si amiable por vendre le moi si chierement au derrien? Tu me fus jadis mere, or m'ies tu devenue marrastre, et por fere moi de duel morir as apelee avec toi la Mort, si que tu en deus manieres m'as honni, de mes amis et de ma terre. Hé! Mort vileinne, tu ne deüsses mie avoir assailli tel home comme mes niés estoit qui de bonté passoit tout le monde.' (172:45–55)

This conception of Fortune, recalling the prisoner's in Boethius's *Consolation*, is shared by many of the characters in the *Mort*. She is a mother-figure when dispensing her secular gifts, but a wicked stepmother when she suddenly withdraws her favours, as Arthur reiterates after the unfortunate killing of Lucan (192:21–24). Similarly she is blamed by Sagremor li Desreez after the slaughter of Yvain by Mordred (190:5–8). Yet both Arthur and Sagremor also imply that God has allowed misfortune to befall them (190:2, 9), the author thus allowing for the possibility that Fortune is God's handmaiden. So, references to an unjust force are juxtaposed with the characters' acknowledgements of their moral responsibility (172:30–32, 40–41; 186:41–46), thus pointing to some human agency in the downfall of King Arthur. The protagonists' contrition and suffering nevertheless elicit sympathy for their untimely demise.

While the characters tend to apportion blame as the final catastrophe approaches, the narrator dissuades us from seeing the carnage as God's punishment of a world become too proud. Just before the battle of Salisbury Plain, he dispels any notion of just deserts when he says: 'Einsi fu emprise la bataille dont meint preudome morurent, qui ne l'avoient pas deservi' (180:1–2). Moreover, it is unlikely that the supernatural events which attend the killing of Mordred imply criticism of Arthur. Mordred, the villain of the later stages of the *Mort*, dies in accordance with the prophecy of the *Lancelot* proper, which cites Arthur's son as the sole cause of everyone's ruin:

> 'car par toi sera mise a destruction la grant hautesce de la Table Reonde et par toi morra li plus preudome que je sache, qui tes peres est. Et tu morras de sa main et ainsi morra li peres par le fil er (*sic*) li filz par le pere.' (XCVI, 23)

Significantly, when the ray of sunlight passing through Mordred's wound is interpreted as 'sygnes de corrouz de Nostre Seigneur' the author seems to distance himself from this gloss by attributing it to the locals: 'cil del païs' (190:58–60). It is even questionable that the term *corrouz* would imply criticism at all, since *corrouz/corrouciez* covers in the *Mort* a range of meanings from anger to distress, grief and a sense of loss (cf. 145:32; 191:3; 192:21–24; 196:8; 197:18). God may well be expressing not so much His displeasure at Arthur but His grief at the tragic killing of son by father and then father by son (191:1–2).

Of all the explanations for Arthur's fall, the one given prominence is that uttered by Fortuna when she appears in his dream on the eve of the battle of Salisbury. In accordance with contemporary iconography, Fortune is depicted with her wheel, on which are seated four great men who are either ascending or descending. Before toppling Arthur from the *regno* (I rule) position at the top of her wheel, she says to the unfortunate king:

> 'Mes tel sont li orgueil terrien qu'il n'i a nul si haut assiz qu'il ne le coviegne cheoir de la poesté del monde.' (176:73–75)

The narrator then comments: 'Einsi vit li rois Artus les mescheances qui li estoient a avenir' (177:1–2). MacRae concludes from Fortune's words that 'the baseness of human actions, then, which overwhelms knightly virtue, and not the whimsical intervention of blind fate' leads to Arthur's rude awakening (*108*, p.276). Yet it is unlikely that 'li orgueil terrien' implies such an unambiguously moral judgement. Fortune, we are told, behaves 'felenessement' towards Arthur (176:76), implying unfair treatment, and the narrator's reference to the misfortunes about to befall him (177:1–2) confirms that we are dealing with Boethian amoral Fortuna (see *135*, pp.105–06). She is presenting the downfall of Arthur's realm as necessary and inevitable, since it is subject to the laws that govern all secular societies. The notion of historical necessity is conveyed by the verb *covenir* (176:74): no ruler, once he has reached these heights, can avoid being toppled. The goddess is thus informing Arthur that the civilisation which bears his name has run its course, for now the Grail adventures have been completed, there is little left for Arthurian knighthood to accomplish. While they still embody admirable secular values 'toutes bones graces por quoi hom puet monter en honneur terriene' (59:62–64), the Knights of the Round Table have no role left to play, except as models for future generations who listen to romances.

The reference to 'li orgueil terrien' (176:73, note the scribal variant in MS *D*: *eür* or 'fortune' for *orgueil*, see *1*, p.201) recalls the *vanitas vanitatum* (vanity of vanities, all is vanity) theme of the Book of Ecclesiastes, whose ethos has much in common with Boethius's *Consolation*. Ecclesiastes emphasises the cyclical nature of life and the importance of timing in the world of man (3:1). It also states that God's time is eternity (3:14), while man's viewpoint is restricted, consequently man is incapable of understanding God's works (11:5). Finally, it argues that there is no justice in this world, no correlation between virtue and reward. The affairs of man are simply ruled by chance:

> the race is not to the swift nor the battle to the strong, nor bread to the wise, nor riches to men of understanding ... For man does not know his time ... men are taken in an evil time, when it falls upon them without warning. (9, 11–12)

A popular biblical text, Ecclesiastes provided contemporaries with another secular way of interpreting the *Mort*.

In transforming Arthurian story into Arthurian history medieval writers employed historiographical models consonant with their view of the past in order to interpret the events of Arthur's life. In contrast to the tendency initiated by Robert de Boron to insert Arthur's reign into Augustinian Salvation History, the *Mort* opted for a more Boethian (and also tragic) model, making Arthurian civilisation subject to the cyclical laws of secular history, symbolised so poignantly by Fortune's wheel. Yet like some contemporary histories, the *Mort* also suggests that the Knights of the Round Table are in part morally responsible for what befalls them, thus contributing to their own demise. This branch of the cycle thus exemplifies the equivocal attitude of many secular writers in the Middle Ages towards the problem of explaining history and the rise and fall of great civilisations (*translatio imperii*). Although there are Christian lessons to be learned, the *Mort* demonstrates *how* and suggests sympathetically *why* Arthur's kingdom did not and could not last for ever. In this respect the author's role resembled that ascribed to Walter Map, who supposedly recorded the events of Arthur's reign (including the *proesces* of his knights) for Henry II and posterity (§1). The *Mort* is thus a tragic narrative with a commemorative function; the Arthurian values it preserved for the scrutiny of posterity will be the subject of Chapter 4.

4. Arthurian Values: condemnation or commemoration?

Although one can read the *Mort* as a tragedy produced by a cleric to commemorate the deeds of Arthur's age (a highpoint in British history), the complexity and ambiguity of the narrative nevertheless leaves scope for more critical, even ironic interpretations. Some critics see in it a demonstration of the vanity of all earthly endeavour and consider that its primary message is religious, showing the superiority of the spiritual over the secular. Others argue that the Knights of the Round Table espouse the wrong ideologies and that Arthur's kingdom relies on outmoded institutions: having reached the decadent phase, Arthurian civilisation deserves to collapse. It is the purpose of this chapter to examine the presentation in the *Mort* of Arthurian institutions and values: the *chevalerie* and *courtoisie* that Wace's Arthur, described in the following quotation, thought worth commemorating:

> Chevaliers fud mult vertüus,
> Mult fud preisanz, mult glorïus ...
> Mult ama *pris*, mult ama *glorie*,
> Mult volt ses faiz metre en memorie.
> Servir se fist curteisement
> E se cuntint mult noblement.
> Tant cum il vesqui et regna,
> Tuz altres princes surmunta
> De curteisie e de noblesce
> E de vertu e de largesce.   (*Brut*, 451–66)

As we saw in Chapter 1, Wace's view of the Arthurian era as exemplary was still in evidence in the *Lancelot* proper. However, in the *Queste*, chivalry inspired by human love and by the hope of increasing one's renown and honour (Wace's *pris* and *glorie*, 1.459

above) is condemned as socially and spiritually destructive, the result of the deadly sin of pride. Here we shall examine the response of the *Mort* to these contrasting traditions.

The Secular and the Spiritual

While noting superficial differences in ethos between the three branches of the *Prose Lancelot*, Frappier still detects a unity of conception and a progression towards greater spirituality. He argues that the *Mort* does not return to the courtly values of the *Lancelot* proper, but instead 'elle répand un voile de tristesse sur les joies et les illusions du *siècle*, et elle se termine après la destruction du monde chevaleresque sur une note d'une religieuse élévation' (*69*, p.398). He sees in Arthur, his knights and the unreformed Lancelot a negative *exemplum* of behaviour which is eclipsed by the positive *exemplum* of the rehabilitated Lancelot gradually renouncing all worldly ties to spend his last years in the service of God (*69*, pp.229–43). Lancelot's woundings, which prevent him from attending tourneys after the Winchester meeting, are interpreted as a sign of God's anger towards this favoured knight for indulging again in the debased form of chivalry that tournaments represent. Moreover, Lancelot's incognito is said to indicate his awareness of the shameful nature of these pursuits (see *89*). Later though, according to Frappier, God strengthens Lancelot's resolve to resist the 'force d'amours', to give up Guinevere, to divest himself of all feudal ties and landed responsibilities, and to earn his salvation.

Although one can detect a general progression from the worldly to the spiritual in the *Mort*, culminating in paragraphs 200–02, there is much in the textual detail to undermine Frappier's arguments (see *107*). First there is no evidence to suggest that Lancelot's incognito is motivated by a sense of guilt. Arthur is surely right when he says that Lancelot attended the Winchester tournament in disguise so that no-one would refuse to fight against him (30:43–48). Lancelot's real concern, to enhance his worldly honour, is revealed when he decides to fight on the weaker side: 'car ce ne seroit pas nostre enneur, se nos aidions a ceus qui en ont le plus bel' (17:12–13). This desire for honour, which Lancelot shares with

Arthur, may be a flaw from the Christian perspective, but the hero's primary motivations at this stage are courtly and chivalric, to serve Guinevere, not to please God. There is no evidence either that the woundings are divine warnings or punishments. Their main function is to keep Lancelot away from court, to enable rumour and misunderstandings to run rife and to force a long separation on the lovers, which inflames their passion. The woundings are treated realistically, which tends to undermine any symbolic interpretation, and the one inflicted by Bohort becomes the subject of some merriment at the latter's expense (§§46–47). As we saw in Chapter 3, the accidental wounding by the huntsman is called 'droite mescheance' (65:27) by the hermit who looks after Lancelot. Although the term can be ambiguous, it is probable that this *preudome* (unlike his predecessors in the *Queste*) is not finding Christian/ethical meanings in every incident that befalls the hero.

Similarly, one could challenge Frappier's contention that Lancelot *chooses* the religious life in preference to the secular and that this process begins when God gives him the fortitude to return Guinevere to Arthur. It is clearly Lancelot's love for the queen (not his Christian piety) which prompts him to renounce her, acting out of concern for her honour:

> 'se vos en fesiez ce que mes cuers desirre, vos remeindriez; mes neporquant, por ce que ge vueill que cist aferes aut plus a vostre enneur que selonc mon desirier, vos en iroiz a vostre seigneur le roi Artu.'
> (118:24–28; cf. *Lancelot*, IX, 33)

This is one of several magnanimous gestures made by Lancelot. Many stem from his Christian conception of chivalry, which requires him to show mercy to defeated fellow knights. Yet his magnanimity is also a product of his love for the queen, from which grows an altruism akin to Christian *caritas*. While the *Queste* presents Lancelot's sinful passion as an obstacle to his salvation, the *Mort* may be suggesting that love for another human being, leading to the sacrifice of one's own desires, is the first step on the ladder towards love of God (a concept known as Neoplatonic gradualism, see *96*).

Although renouncing Guinevere paves the way for Lancelot's repentance and salvation, the knight turns to the religious life only when all of his worldly obligations have been fulfilled (see *151*, pp.36–37). Not until Guinevere is dead and Mordred's sons have been punished for Arthur's death, does Lancelot turn to God (see *107*, p.145). After Lyonel's death, the narrator reports of Lancelot that 'or ne li estoit il riens remés, quant il avoit perdu sa dame et son cousin' (199:24–25). Lancelot's decision to spend his last days with his companions, with whom he had shared the 'deliz del siecle' (200:41), is marked more by joy at their reunion than heartfelt repentance (§200), though he devotes himself wholeheartedly to penance later (201:28–33; 202:33–38). Lancelot, like Gawain, supervises the manner in which he will be remembered by posterity. He chooses to be buried at Joyeuse Garde next to Galeholt (202:4–7), thus reaffirming the emotional links with his best friend from the *Lancelot* proper, and with his lover Guinevere, in whose name he originally won the castle. Moreover his epitaph stresses that he dies a knight not a priest (203:16–19).

Guinevere's choice of the religious life is not prompted by spirituality either. She enters the convent for her own safety and the abbess's compromise solution to the queen's predicament suggests a greater concern for Arthur's wishes than for God's (§170). On her husband's death and out of fear of Mordred's sons Guinevere 'prist maintenant les dras de la religion' (195:20). This is no great spiritual conversion; yet it does prepare the way for her pious death, and there is no detectable irony in the narrator's comment 'mes onques haute dame plus bele fin n'ot ne plus bele repentance, ne plus doucement criast merci a Nostre Seigneur qu'ele fist' (197:14–17). Here more allowance is being made for human frailty than in the *Queste*, which condemns Guinevere's sin.

If, as Frappier maintains, the *Mort* does not embrace the ethos of the *Lancelot* proper, but forms a fitting sequel instead to the *Queste,* then the behaviour of Bohort in the final branch is strikingly inconsistent. For, as Frappier admits (*69*, pp.326–28), he seems to

Arthurian Values: condemnation or commemoration?

suffer from amnesia after his spiritual experiences on the Grail quest and reverts to exclusively worldly activities until his entry into the hermitage on Lancelot's death (§204). Before then his religious observance is mentioned only once, in a perfunctory manner: 'tant que Lancelos fu levez et qu'il ot oïe messe, et li dui roi [Lyonnel and Bohort] ausi' (145:5–6). Some may argue that Bohort's return to worldly values simply reflects Arthurian post-quest decadence, which God punishes in the final debacle. However, there is no evidence that the author disapproves of the more secular Bohort, he simply has a different conception of him. Bohort is a very great and courageous knight, who makes an excellent match for Lancelot at the Winchester tournament, but then suffers the embarrassment of wounding him, thus becoming the butt of Gawain's cruel jokes (§46–47). His excellent prowess is again displayed at the tournaments of Taneborc (§43) and Camelot, which he wins (66:9). Later Bohort slays Guerrehet, admittedly after issuing a *défi* (94:29–30), but this act would not have been condoned in the *Queste*. Moreover, he is less generous and merciful than Lancelot, regretting that the latter did not kill Gawain during the single combat (158:15–17). He also urges Lancelot before they both turn to piety to avenge Arthur's death on Mordred's sons (§196). His attitude to Lancelot's love for Guinevere hardly befits the chaste hero of the *Queste* either. Although he disapproves of the adultery (59:13–17), he nevertheless tries to persuade Guinevere to take her lover back (§59, see Chapter 5), and worries that Lancelot will regret returning her to Arthur (§118:42–54). So, in keeping with the characterisation technique of the *Mort*, Bohort is a nuanced figure, embodying more humane, chivalric and courtly values than his counterpart in the *Queste*. He emblematises the cycle's return to secular ideology, dedicating himself to the spiritual, like Lancelot, only when there is no role left for him to play in Arthurian politics.

Feudal Values in Crisis?

While accepting that character flaws do not explain the demise of Arthurian society, R. Howard Bloch (*37–40*) argues that the degradation of courtly and chivalric ideals and the ineffectiveness of feudal institutions precipitate its end. The thirteenth-century author projected onto Arthur's world a contemporary ideological crisis and in criticising in particular a judicial system consisting of capture *in flagrante delicto*, trial by combat and vendetta, he was demonstrating its inferiority to the new inquisitorial system being developed in France.

Since the *Mort* was composed during a period when the Church's disapproval of the *judicium Dei* culminated in the prohibitions of the fourth Lateran Council in 1215, it is not surprising that it reflects contemporary judicial and theological debate. Opponents criticised the trial by combat's dependence on luck (the ability to find a champion in time) and chivalric excellence (the possibility of might triumphing over right) and these concerns are expressed by several characters in the *Mort* (74:98–03; 85:9–11; but cf. 144:61–74). However, the romance needs to be read also within the context of literary tradition (see Muir, *121*), and by focusing on the narrative function of the two judicial duels, one realises that, like Beroul in his *Tristran*, the author is making important, yet controversial, moral distinctions: between action and intention, and between the spirit and the letter of the law (cf. *79*).

In the poisoned fruit episode the intention of the queen is not always taken into account (compare 62:52–57; 67:95 with 67:64–65, 90–91; 72:15). However, she is ultimately tried on the question of motivation, and as she did not intend to kill Gaheris, the outcome is presented as just. Lancelot's willingness to defend the queen is not condemned, for he is motivated by a noble sentiment: his selfless love for her (75:33–42). Moreover, his triumph over Mador is justified by the emphasis on intention (83:4–5) and on the known 'valeur' of the queen (82:21–26, see *126*). Gawain predicts and approves the outcome:

> 'Or creroie ge bien que Mador fust en mauvese querele;
> car comment que ses freres moreust, je jurroie seur seinz
> au mien escient qu'onques la reïne n'i pensa desloiauté
> ne traïson.' (83:9–12)

Arthurian Values: condemnation or commemoration? 73

I disagree with Bloch when he suggests that Lancelot *cynically* manipulates judicial formulae (*37*, p.46). Instead, the author is drawing a sophisticated (and, at the time, rare) distinction between action and intention, thus reflecting contemporary theological debate on the nature of sin. An inquisitorial system based on signed testimony (which Bloch claims the author favoured) would, in Guinevere's case, have led to her false conviction, since all witnesses saw her hand over the fruit.

In the second combat between Lancelot and Gawain right triumphs, for Lancelot is in the morally superior position (148:76–83), having tried to avoid bloodshed with the offer of generous reparations. Besides, he is not guilty of *traïson* or murder of an underhand kind since he killed Gaheriet unknowingly: 'onques au mien escient n'ocis Gaheriet' (147:85–86; cf. 94:54), and Agravain openly in a fair fight (94:2–27). Trusting in God's justice (148:29), he nevertheless fears failure, since he has actually killed two of Gawain's brothers: 'car moult doutoit qu'il ne li mescheïst envers monseigneur Gauvain por la mort de ses freres qu'il avoit ocis' (149:15–17). Thus although the distinction between right and wrong is not always clear-cut for the protagonists, the author employs the *judicium Dei* in the *Mort* to apply a greater justice than that meted out by mere human agency.

Bloch's contention that the trial by combat does not 'prevent the violence of private grievance from menacing and destroying the integrity of the realm' (*37*, p.54) is also untrue, for after the first duel Mador drops his suit, and the second duel not only avoids unnecessary bloodshed, but also resolves the conflict between the families of Arthur and King Ban. Instead, Roman aggression and Mordred's treachery precipitate the catastrophe. There are grounds for criticism in Arthur's pursuit of Lancelot to Gaunes after the deaths of his nephews, turning a private family vendetta into a public war. However, the attempt to punish Lancelot for adultery and to win back Guinevere is justified, for adultery with a queen is not 'a private offense to the royal family' (*38*, p.299), but treason (86:47). The queen's infidelity, like Iseut's in Beroul's *Tristran*, not only threatens Arthur's bloodline, but also dangerously undermines the respect due to the king from his subjects and enemies (see Morgan's words, 53:66–68).

Bloch maintains that the deaths of Gawain's brothers 'initiate an endless cycle of vendetta and war — Gauvain against Lancelot, Arthur against Mordret, Lancelot against the sons of Mordret' (*38*, p.293) and sees their desire for 'clannish vengeance' as undermining the security of Logres. This is true only for the pursuit of Lancelot to Gaunes. Gawain's grievance is resolved by the duel with Lancelot and although criticism of Arthur is implied when he refuses to ask for Lancelot's help against Mordred, there is no condemnation of Arthur's desire to punish his treacherous son. Furthermore, Lancelot and 'tuit li autre bon chevalier de Gaunes' (196:9–10) win narratorial approval when they decide to avenge Arthur's death on Mordred's sons. This is not a case of 'clannish vengeance', but revenge motivated by love and justice.

A final criticism levelled against Arthurian society by Bloch is that the feudal system itself contributes to the illustrious king's downfall. It is, he maintains, the vertical hierarchy of allegiance, in which a vassal owes loyalty to his immediate superior rather than promoting the national good, that enables Mordred to usurp power from Arthur. This system based on personal loyalty to the king is, of course, at its most vulnerable when the monarch leaves the country on campaign. There is a tradition in Arthurian literature of treachery in such cases (see Chrétien's *Cligés*) and one of the *données* of the sources is that Arthur is betrayed while abroad. The questions raised by the *Mort* are: does Arthur show a lack of judgement in choosing Mordred as regent? Is Arthurian society flawed in that it is vulnerable to treachery? When Gawain suggests finding someone in whose keeping to leave the queen Arthur seems at a loss whom to choose, until Mordred volunteers and Arthur gladly accepts. This is a mistake, as Guinevere realises (129:19–24), for Arthur is more blind to Mordred's character flaws than the queen (and he seems to have forgotten his prophetic dream, §164). Nevertheless, as Zuurdeeg argues (*158*, p.72) Mordred has some fine qualities (139:24–27; 140:13–17; 168:13, 46–47; 188:8, 19–21, 32–33), thus rendering Arthur's choice less obviously foolhardy. Handing over the keys to the treasury and asking his subjects to swear an oath of fealty to Mordred (actions criticised by Bloch) are necessary practical steps to enable the regent to support Arthur abroad, though the narrator remarks that the king will regret this action (129:25–36). The treacherous loyalty shown by Arthur's subjects to Mordred is not merely the result of this oath; his son buys greater support with generous and frequent gifts (134:7–12; 168:10–25), Arthur thus becoming a victim of Judas-like betrayal. When, however, the barons of Logres swear a further oath to help Mordred against his enemies and (most shockingly) even against Arthur were he to turn up (142:60–64), they do so because they believe that the king and Gawain have been killed by Lancelot and everyone fears the return of the queen's lover and his likely usurpation of the throne. Rather than condemning the feudal system itself, the *Mort* is castigating the unspeakable treachery of Mordred (who claims that his own father is dead and who tries to marry his father's wife) and probably also the unreliablity and gullibility of Arthur's subjects (who later support Mordred's sons too, 196:51–52). Indeed, it is questionable that any political system is immune to treachery. In arguing that the author promotes the idea of a centralised national monarchy to curb the power of the feudal nobility, Bloch's position is diametrically opposed to critics who see in the *Mort* a critique of thirteenth-century kings' increasing power (see *46–48*).

While the legal/feudal institutions operating in the *Mort* are not as flawed as Bloch maintains, conflicts of allegiance based on personal, family or feudal ties are destructive of the Arthurian world (see *158*). Lancelot above all is torn by love and loyalty to Guinevere, to his kin, to Arthur's family, and to fellow Knights of the Round Table. His feudal allegiance to Arthur is unclear — deliberately so to exculpate Lancelot from grave charges of treason (see *48*, p.47). For much of the *Lancelot* proper the eponymous hero is not really the king's vassal, but Guinevere's knight. Towards the end of that branch Arthur claims to have given Lancelot Gaul (*Lancelot*, CV, 15), yet later Lancelot refuses the crown (CV, 27). In the *Mort*, Lancelot can challenge Arthur from the Joyeuse Garde because the castle does not constitute a fief; he then divests himself of any land before going to France (125:7-15, see *33*, p.38). Lancelot's conflicting bonds are therefore emotional (love and friendship) rather than strictly legal and thus enhance the tragedy of the *Mort*.

Whereas the divided loyalties experienced by Lancelot and Arthur stem from laudable qualities tragically brought into conflict, the family antagonism which is unleashed by the war between Arthur and Lancelot is less excusable. The seeds of this antagonism are evident early in the *Mort*. Hector leaps too readily and angrily to Bohort's defence when Arthur tells the latter that he will regret wounding the anonymous knight at the Winchester tournament: 'Et Hestors, qui cuide que li rois ait dite ceste parole par mal de Boort, saut avant toz corrouciez et pleins de mautalent' (24:34-36). Lancelot's family stays at Arthur's court only out of love for Lancelot: 'Et sachiez veraiement, dame, fet Boorz, que nos n'eüssons mie tant demoré en cest païs comme nos avons, se por l'amor de mon seigneur ne fust, ne il n'i eüst pas tant demoré aprés la queste del Seint Graal fors por vos' (36:59-64), so when the queen's love turns to anger, Bohort and clan soon depart. Although Bohort realises that Lancelot's happiness depends on his continued relationship with the queen, he clearly disapproves of her (§59) and he and Hector feel sure that the queen will be the cause of war between the families (66:48-54).

Bohort's concern for Lancelot also leads him to make Guinevere suffer during the poisoned fruit episode, as punishment for her unfair treatment of his cousin (§§77-78). Yet equally out of love for their kinsman, both Hector and Bohort are prepared to fight in defence of the queen (74:117-20; 75:29-32), while Gawain refuses, despite Arthur's entreaties (79:8-23). Ties of kinship can therefore have positive consequences. Similarly, there are several occasions during the war between Arthur and Lancelot when personal bonds of friendship and love between the two opponents nearly avert disaster. Unfortunately, the king is goaded on by Gawain, and the descendants of King Ban are full of vengeful hatred (112:57-58; 114:39-43; 115:124-29; 147:12-14; 148:37-43; 158:6-8). Nevertheless, the *Mort* ends on a note of unity as Bohort and his family avenge

Arthurian Values: condemnation or commemoration?

Arthur's death as if it were a personal matter: 'nos ne veons mie comment nos en puissons estre vengié autrement' (197:20). Thus, paradoxically, Lancelot's love for Guinevere (and for Arthur too) has succeeded in uniting the two families.

Arthurian Ideology

The values on which Arthurian chivalry and courtesy were based, and on which the feudal and judicial systems also depended, were loyalty, honour, truthfulness, nobility (of birth and character), justice, courage and generosity (largesse). These secular qualities were ideally accompanied by the Christian virtues of mercy, humility (in specific cicumstances) and love (*caritas*). The main characters in the *Mort* are all of noble birth, the lower orders rarely mentioned (113:24–25). Even the demoiselle d'Escalot is deemed by some to be too lowly for Lancelot, yet a vavassor's daughter belonged to the lesser nobility (see *124*). In general, they embody positive traits, vices being reserved for Morgan, Mordred, Agravain and those of Arthur's barons who support Mordred. Although the narrator intervenes rarely to express approval or disapproval, epithets implying positive value judgements abound in the *Mort* (see *6*). Statistics are no substitute for literary analysis, but it is striking to note that occurrences of positive terms such as *amor* (100), *amer* (143), *ami* (30), *bon* (161), *bonté* (10), *bien* (526; but problematic as the term is often a mere intensifier), *biens* (13), *beau* (159), *bel* (10), *biauté* (10), *debonere* (7), *debonerté* (7), *droit* (noun 34; adjective 15), *halt* (70), *hardi* (23), *loial* (8), *loiaument* (15), *loiauté* (4), *preu* (noun 6, adj. 12), *preudom* (123), *proesce* (27) far outweigh the use of negatives: *desloialté* (21), *desloiaument* (7), *desloiauter* (4), *desmesure* (1), *fol* (16), *folement* (3), *folie* (5), *haïne* (10), *haïr* (27), *honte* (46), *honir* (39), *mal* (adv. 12, adj. 8, noun 24), *malvés* (18), *malvestié* (1), *orgueill* (3), *orgueillex* (1), *outrage* (5). *Chevalerie* (25) and *chevalier* (440) are most often accompanied by the positive adjectives *bon*, *haut*, *grant*, *loial* or *fort*, rarely by *fol*, and only once by *felon* and *mauvés coarz* (*6*, pp.267–76). While terms denoting *courtoisie* are rare (*cortoisie* 3, *cortois* 4), the author is particularly interested in the feudal virtues of honour (*aneur* 66) and loyalty (27 occurrences of related terms). Szkilnik (*149*) demonstrates how subjective the concepts of loyalty and treason are in the *Mort*, occurring as they do mainly in direct speech and thus representing the views of one character on another. The lovers are frequently accused of treason, but mostly by the ill-intentioned characters Mordred, Morgan and Agravain, who are the only ones to be termed disloyal by the narrator. Szkilnik concludes that the work sets up a conflict between moral loyalty (exemplified by Lancelot towards Arthur) and vassalic fidelity, which merely follows the letter of the law in disclosing the adultery to the king (a distinction made by Gawain, 87:59–61). Close semantic analysis thus reveals the text's questioning of key values and its refusal to encourage facile moral judgements on the behaviour of Arthurian heroes. In fact, one response the work seems to be encouraging is that of amazement, wonder, even admiration, judging from the frequency of words related to the marvellous and extraordinary: *merveille* (40), *merveillex* (20), *merveilleusement* (7), *merveiller* (26). This conclusion is supported by Chênerie's work on the honorific term *preudome* in the *Mort*, whose general tone and use of epithets recalls the panegyric or funeral eulogy: 'ce roman, qui semble raconter avec la mort du roi, la fin d'un monde idéal, développe en réalité un véritable panégyrique du héros chevaleresque et courtois' (*58*, p.82). What then are the values being reassessed, praised and commemorated?

Admiration (which sixteenth-century theorists identified as part of the tragic response, *102*, p.3) is clearly being elicited in the *Mort* for Arthurian prowess, represented by the king and his knights despite the fact that the Round Table now comprises only 72 of its original 150 members (107:25–28). Arthur, a far more active king than the *roi fainéant* of Chrétien's later romances (see *141*) is praised by the narrator during the siege of Joyeuse Garde for his fighting skills:

> Et celui jor porta li rois Artus armes et le fist si bien qu'il
> n'a el monde home de son aage qui ausi bien le poïst
> avoir fet. (115:103–05)

'L'estoire' tells us that he was an inspiration to his men (115:106–10), an ability he shares with Lancelot and one prized by other medieval writers recording exemplary acts for emulation. Arthur's contribution to the victory against the Romans is again glorious (§161), the narrator's admiration for chivalry extending even to the Roman emperor (161:50–52). Similarly, Lancelot's excellence in feats of arms is frequently admired, this quality enabling others to identify him as a *preudom*, despite his incognito (12:29, 44; 19:18–21). (Interestingly, the term *preudome*, which in the *Queste* designates pious, educated hermits, refers in the *Mort* to worthy, brave fighters, another indication of a different ethos.) Lancelot's chivalric deeds are described enthusiastically, even when he is fighting his fellow Knights of the Round Table:

> Et Lancelos...met la main a l'espee et commence a doner
> granz cox destre et senestre et a abatre chevaliers et a
> ocirre chevax et a esrachier escuz de cox et hiaumes de
> testes et a fere granz proesces de toutes parz, si que nus
> nel voit qui nel tiengne a grant merveille. (20:1–7)

The narrator is just as approving of Bohort and Hector:'le commencent si bien a fere a leur endroit que nus nes en peüst a droit blasmer' (20:8–10), while Guinevere is presented as an admirer of feats of arms (7:8–10). Arthurian knights inspire prowess in their brothers-in-arms (20:10–14) and nowhere are their actions explicitly criticised. Later, during the battle of Salisbury, the narrator laments the death of Yvain saying: 'ce fu domajes doulereus, quar a celi termine tenoit l'en monseigneur Yvain a un des bons chevaliers qui fust el monde et au plus preudomme' (189:31–34). Even as their pious ends approach, Lancelot and his cousin Bohort pursue the sons of Mordred with vigour, Bohort fighting 'comme cil qui meint grant cop avoit doné' (197:42) so that 'nus ne le voit qui ne s'en merveille' (197:51–52). When news of Arthur's death reaches Lancelot, the narrator comments that he is 'molt corrouciez' (his distress creating pathos) and so are 'tuit li autre bon chevalier de Gaunes' (196:8–10). The term *bon* implies approval not just of Lancelot and his men, but also of their plan to avenge Arthur. As I argued earlier, revenge rather than withdrawal to concentrate on Christian salvation seems entirely appropriate here. The *Queste*'s disapproval of worldly chivalry is absent from the *Mort*, although there may be glimpses of contemporary church criticism of tourneying in the depiction of unnecessary bloodshed at tournaments (21:10–13; see *97*). Lancelot's secular chivalry is nevertheless presented as if it were sacred. Its symbolic representation, Lancelot's shield, is first seen by Gawain hanging in a room full of candles, reminiscent of a shrine (§27) and later it is venerated, like a relic (121:10), in the Church of St Stephen in Camelot, where Lancelot first received 'l'ordre de chevalerie' (120:21, cf. 12:10–13). Despite the religious terminology, Lancelot is explicit in wanting his shield to commemorate his *secular* chivalry: 'si que tuit cil qui des ore mes le verront aient en remenbrance les merveilles que ge ai fetes en ceste terre' (120:17–19). Although Lancelot's epitaph (203:16–19) and the words of King Yon (104:11–13) imply that Lancelot's achievements have been surpassed by his more spiritual son, the *Mort* responds to the *Queste*'s denigration of Lancelot's secular chivalry by reminding us of the glorious feats of this worldly knight, whose prestige is enhanced further by begetting Galahad.

The male protagonists are expected not just to be good Christian warriors, attending mass before battle, but also good leaders of men. Both Lancelot (§199) and Arthur (§98–99) exhibit the *sensibilité* associated with military leaders when mourning their dead; they avenge the deaths of their companions in battle, Arthur praying for their souls (191:37–39). Both inspire loyalty in their vassals, although Arthur has to require a special oath of fealty from his men before pursuing Lancelot abroad (104:67–71). In contrast, Lancelot has men flocking to join him, from the young knights of Escalot who become his companions and vassals (16:13–18; 56:15–24; see *110*, p.8) to the people of Joyeuse Garde and environs who greet his arrival as if it were the second coming of Christ: 'si li vindrent a l'encontre ausi grant joie fesant com se ce fust Dex meïsmes' (97:24–25). His men's loyalty is absolute (149:33–38).

Arthurian Values: condemnation or commemoration?

Another characteristic of the exemplary leader of men is his willingness to take advice. Lancelot requests and heeds advice from Bohort and Lyonel before embarking on war (115:14–16; 196:10–11). Arthur, on the other hand, asks for advice (the feudal duty of *consilium*), but takes the wrong kind. Indeed, in the extended council before the siege of Joyeuse Garde, when Yon advises restraint in the interests, not of the king's honour, but of the kingdom (104:6–20), Arthur is only too willing to accede to the bellicose urgings of Mordred and Mador. Later, he does little consulting, following either his own inclinations or those of Gawain. This has led Boutet to see in the portrayal of Arthur a criticism of kings who refused to take seriously the feudal duty of consultation, his susceptibility to bad advice recalling the weak kings in the Old French epic of revolt (*46–48*). The *Mort* may indeed reflect the concerns of thirteenth-century French nobles angered by increasing royal power. Thus, the work could constitute a form of literary revenge on overweening and inflexible monarchs (see *46–48; 110*).

Whatever Arthur's shortcomings, he is not an unjust king. He follows the correct judicial procedure when Mador de la Porte, breaking his vassalic bond by returning his land to the king (67:57–62), accuses the queen of treason. Arthur allows Guinevere the customary 40 days to find a champion (68:23–38), but since he functions as judge, cannot fight on her behalf. Despite his distress when he fails to recruit Gawain for her defence (79:8–29), Arthur does not attempt to pervert the course of justice. Mador's accusation of trickery against the king is unfounded, his objection to Lancelot as opponent merely revealing his doubts concerning God's defence of right in judicial combats (85:9–11). Arthur does, however, act illegally in deciding to burn Guinevere for adultery and in countenancing no objection from his barons (92:42–50; 93:6–17), but yet again he is humanised by his capacity for pity (93:44–47).

Both Arthur and Lancelot are motivated by honour, a concept no longer closely linked to land-holding, but to the thirteenth-century nobility's sense of lineage and social superiority. In the *Mort* the term *aneur* (66 occurrences, see *6*) is associated with the good reputation and chivalric accolades which noble knights can win for themselves (17:12), and the loss of honour is unacceptable (*honte* and *honir* occurring 46 & 39 times respectively). When Guinevere is abducted Arthur's personal shame is at issue, as is demonstrated by the lengthy war-council with his barons. However, as Gawain reminds the king, he needs to protect his honour for the benefit of his whole family: 'si seriez honis et vostres lignages abaissiés, si que vous n'avriés jamais honour, se vous faisiés pais a Lancelot' (110:19–22). Similarly, Lancelot is keen to preserve family honour when fighting against Arthur and Gawain (115:12–14; 145:42). Several characters are unable to renege on oaths uttered in moments of crisis (90:21–23) and honour can become problematic. It is because Lancelot is an honourable man that he will not break his word to the demoiselle d'Escalot, despite his intimation of disaster (§14), and Arthur, in avenging his shame, risks the well-being of his kingdom. The *Mort* thus demonstrates how Arthurian virtues can, in certain circumstances, have disastrous consequences.

Arthurian society is characterised by *courtoisie*, which takes many forms. Arthur's discretion in not betraying Lancelot's anonymity is courtly (24:16–20), so is Lancelot's expression of emotion (111:5–11), although grieving should be moderated (2:7–9), and grief dissimulated in order to keep up morale (111:34–35; 126:10–14). Lancelot's courtesy involves politeness to ladies and hospitable hosts (§§14, 15 & 38), and complete obedience to Guinevere (89:23–26): he always seeks the queen's permission before embarking on a course of action, even when rescuing her from the stake (95:8–9; cf. 8:8–15; 90:50–55), and he behaves as a courtly lover in exchanging love tokens when they part (119:3–11). Gawain, the *chevalier courtois par excellence* of Arthurian romance, proves his *courtoisie* in the demoiselle d'Escalot episode. An expert in verbal courtship, he humbly withdraws when he discovers that Lancelot is his rival (§27), nevertheless offering the girl his loyal service (30:10–15). However, the courtly qualities of both knights provoke fatal passions, and the association of sexual love with death is a disturbing feature of the *Mort*. The first example is the demoiselle d'Escalot. Her infatuation for Lancelot seems fated from the very beginning (38:79–81; 39:19–20: 'car il m'est ensi destiné que je muire por lui'), her death epitomising the dangers of *courtoisie*. The second case involves the dame de Beloé (§174), an episode in which Maurice considers Gawain to be a posthumous 'ferment de discorde' (*110*, p.68). Yet her death serves as much to enhance Gawain's reputation as it does to criticise the effects of immoderate passion. Indeed, envy and hatred incite the lord of Beloé (174:3–7) to kill his wife, as well as her distress at Gawain's passing (174:15–22). In both cases, the object of desire unwittingly causes the lady's demise, creating pathos rather than moral condemnation.

Using the technique of displacement, the author of the *Mort* links love and killing metaphorically, but this link complicates rather than aids interpretation. Thus, when Lancelot is accused by the demoiselle d'Escalot of *vilenie* in her letter, he may be innocent of her death, but guilty of cuckolding the king, who significantly reads the letter (§71). Similarly, although Lancelot and Guinevere are never put on trial for their adultery, they are both accused of killing (see *86, 126*). The murders of Gaheris and Gaheriet are unintentional, yet the poisoned fruit may deliberately evoke Eve's apple and thus link Guinevere with female sin. However, the issue of culpability is complicated rather than resolved by the analogy, for emphasis on intention during the judicial combats exonerates the defendants of their false crime, thus rendering their true crime morally ambiguous. Kay rightly concludes that in the *Mort* adultery is the 'ethical expression' of 'human mortality and frailty' (*86*, p.42), although I disagree that the work's humaneness is pessimistic. One could further argue that criticism of Lancelot's adultery is also displaced onto Mordred's illicit desire for Guinevere, implying that both men dishonour Arthur equally (163:34–35). However, the differences between Lancelot and Mordred are legion. There is no courtly relationship, entered into freely by consenting adults, between Mordred and Guinevere. Furthermore, Lancelot, in loving the queen, shows no desire to usurp Arthur's throne (see *126*). In contrast, Mordred treats the queen as symbolic of the land of Logres, both needing to be seized to underpin his kingship. Thus, Lancelot gains in moral stature from comparison with his rival.

Although, like many other themes in the *Mort*, sexual love is treated ambiguously (its creative and destructive sides both being illustrated, *158*, p.19) Lancelot's passion for the queen is nevertheless a noble, self-sacrificing love. As Santucci shows, the conjugal love of Arthur and Guinevere is also portrayed positively (130:4–15; 136:8–12), along with several examples of love and friendship between men (*140*). The bonds of *compagnonnage* and male affection are illustrated by many of the knights, but particularly by Arthur, Lancelot and Gawain, whose earlier friendship makes their enmity all the more moving (§88). However, it is Lancelot alone who exemplifies the magnanimity or *caritas* expected of a Christian knight. He shows mercy to Mador de la Porte, first by dismounting (84:28–30), then by offering to have him pardoned (84:50–56), actions described as *debonereté* and *franchise* (85:1–2). Then he allows Arthur's army to rest before battle (109:4–8) and refuses to hurt Arthur (115:115–31; 116:1–4), earning the king's praise and even regret over the war: 'ore a il passez de bonté et de cortoisie touz les chevaliers que ge onques veïsse; or voudroie ge que ceste guerre n'eüst onques esté commenciee, car plus a hui veincu mon cuer par deboneretè que touz li monz n'eüst par force' (116:8–13). Later Lancelot tries to avoid single combat with Gawain, vowing never to kill him, 'car trop me samble prodom et si est li hom el monde qui riens ne m'est que je plus ai amé et aim encore, fors le roi solement' (145:69–72), and offering him very advantage-ous peace conditions (147:49–90). That these are rejected by Gawain reflects badly on him, and Lancelot emerges as the true Christian hero, abandoning the combat to save his opponent (§157). Curiously though, Lancelot's love for Arthur and his nephew makes us view them in a more sympathetic light too, as knights deserving of Lancelot's love and respect. And a further factor which mitigates their intransigent behaviour, as we saw in Chapter 2, is their tragic loss of kin.

I hope to have shown that the *Mort* contains many laudable Arthurian values which the author felt worthy of commemoration. However, just as noble characters can behave reprehensibly when pushed to the brink by misfortune, so values such as honour, courtesy, chivalry and love can, when misplaced or brought into

Arthurian Values: condemnation or commemoration?

conflict by bad luck, lead to tragic consequences. When it comes to judging the actions and ethical codes of the protagonists the *Mort* offers no easy solutions. Indeed, its ambiguity encourages a *remise en question* not only of Arthurian ideals, but also of our methods for making moral judgements and for arriving at the truth. According to Delcourt (*62*), the narrative is structured like a labyrinth, through which Arthur and his knights wander, trying to make sense of the conflicting evidence before them. Nothing is quite what it seems. Some characters speak the truth while aiming to deceive; others lie for the general good. Clearly the thirteenth-century author shared with Beroul a familiarity with Peter Abelard's writings on the role of intention in sinning and lying (see *79*). Moreover, as we shall see in Chapter 5, the *Mort*'s very structure reflects the method, pioneered by Abelard and practised in the thirteenth-century universities, of juxtaposing contradictories which require examination and questioning through the application of logic. So the final branch of the Vulgate Cycle challenges the prevailing legal system, which privileged action over intention; it questions the bases of human knowledge — can we know people by their actions? Should we rely on the evidence of our hearts rather than our eyes? It undermines the essentialist view of character held by Arthur and many a medieval writer, whereby good characters cannot behave in a treacherous manner. Lancelot can, but this does not make him a traitor. Above all, the use of ambiguity, indirection, even obfuscation (see *86*) obliges each reader to share with Arthur the adventure of the labyrinth.

5. The Art of the Prose Romancer

Style and Language

For those familiar with the rhetorical sophistication of Chrétien de Troyes's verse, the prose style of the *Mort* may appear somewhat bald and repetitive. The Vulgate Cycle represents one of the earliest experiments in prose and its self presentation as a (hi)story which narrates itself may partly account for its often legalistically verbose reporting of events and largely unembellished narrative style. However, lyrical beauty is achieved in its many laments, while dialogue is employed to great dramatic effect. There is a rhythmic quality to the narrative proper, while the all-pervasive irony creates some humour and much tragic pathos.

Frappier has shown that the author of the *Mort* uses a restricted range of vocabulary, favouring vague expressions over technical terms (an exception being judicial language and some courtly vocabulary) and employing a wordy, repetitive style. For instance, his favourite phrase for conveying loud noises, 'que on n'i oïst pas Dieu tonnant', occurs at least three times in the last thirty paragraphs (173:8–9; 185:55–56; 202:50). Although the inflexion of thirteenth-century French allowed for considerable flexibility in word order, the *Mort* usually places the verb in second position after either the subject or complement in both main and subordinate clauses. Only occasionally (notably in relative clauses) is an unusual word order employed for emphasis: e.g. 'que tel i perdront qui deservi ne l'avoient pas' (59:14–15). Nevertheless, the author's syntax is highly expressive, affective and rhythmic (see *69*, pp. 378–79).[2]

---

[2] It should be noted that Frappier's textual references in *69*, pp.347–97, give the *page* numbers of his 1936 edition.

The Art of the Prose Romancer

Rychner (*137–38*) observes that there is little description or commentary in the *Mort* and, focusing on narrative, he analyses the three methods employed to begin a sentence. These are: temporal phrases (e.g. 'quant...si'); dramatic phrases usually naming the agent of the action (e.g. 'Et Lancelos') and the term 'si' which links a sentence to the previous one predicatively. The narrative proceeds paratactically; events are narrated in sequence (or two sequences if *entrelacement* is present, see below, *Structure and Meaning*) with little subordination and few logical or causal connectives:

> il est remarquable que **les relations logiques**, l'hypothèse, la cause, la concession, la conséquence, le but, **ne jouent qu'un rôle infime dans l'enchaînement des procès principaux**.' (*137*, p.235)

Although the features listed by Rychner in the above quotation are present in the *Mort*, they are not used to link sentences, the conjunction *mais* occurring most frequently, but not with great contrastive force. While temporal phrases can imply causality, since an action may be caused by a preceding one, they do not spell out causation, which often has to be supplied by the reader.

Two types of temporal phrase are particularly significant. The type exemplified by 'celui jor' indicates that an event is being linked to a previous one through chronological proximity; incidents are thereby related to the overall plot, i.e. to romance time rather than objective time. Phrases such as 'au soir' imply a chronology independent of the protagonists, although these may simply be devices to enable the reader to follow the interlaced plot (see *69*, pp.351–60). Indications of timing may also reflect the author's interest in the practicalities of military campaigns. However, Imbs, comparing allusions to hours in the day in the *Queste* and *Mort*, concludes that time is subjective and symbolic in the former, more objective and 'modern' in the latter (*83*, p.293). Indeed, the treatment of time in the *Mort* is not only realistic, but thematic, for an objective chronology implies that the protagonists operate in an impersonal world, which renders them victims of adverse timing.

Whereas there are more references to precise times and real places in the *Mort* than in the *Queste*, thus creating a veneer of realism, there is little physical description of geographical locations or characters. The portrayal of Morgan's castle concentrates on the marvellous nature of Arthur's surroundings, the bright sunshine on the day he reads the pictures perhaps symbolic of enlightenment (§51). There are no detailed descriptions of courtly pomp and luxury which characterise verse romance, and lovers, whose attractions are traditionally described in elaborate rhetorical portraits, remain physically ill-defined. Guinevere's beauty is accepted as a *donnée* of Arthurian literature, and the demoiselle d'Escalot receives no portrait even when she becomes the object of Gawain's desire. Although some characters have already been described earlier in the cycle (e.g. Gawain's brothers in *Lancelot*, LXIX, 1–7) the lack of physical individualisation of both male and female protagonists in the *Mort* suggests that the author's interests lie elsewhere.

Men are, however, described through their actions, and the battle scenes receive particularly detailed attention. We learn first of the division of armies into battalions led by named heroes, whose fates will be related (180:19–26, note that Mordred's battalions are sketched more impersonally in §181, thus eliciting less audience sympathy for their destruction). The fighting itself is enlivened by passages of dialogue, which individualise the combatants and create pathos when a knight, on whom the narrative has just focused, meets his end. A good example is the conversation between Yon and Yvain, in which the latter admits his fear of death. When Yon is shortly afterwards killed by an Irishman, Yvain poignantly laments his passing and predicts the end of the Round Table fellowship (§183). A further dramatic device, borrowed from epic poetry, is the repetition of the deictic phrase 'si poïssiez veoir' (185:33; 190:14, 26; 198:27) which makes readers feel more involved in the action. Combat is described with much hyperbole or epic exaggeration to emphasise the extraordinary prowess of the fighters, their great suffering and the wasteful slaughter of so many fine men:

The Art of the Prose Romancer

> la poïssiez veoir a l'assembler meint biau coup de lance
> et meint bon chevalier a la terre verser, et meint bon
> cheval corre tout estraié parmi le champ, qu'il n'estoit
> qui les retenist; si poïssiez veoir en poi d'eure la terre
> couverte de chevaliers dont li un estoient mort et li autre
> navré. (181:45–51)

Binomial expressions or doublets (the linking of pairs of synonyms) are a feature of the author's style (85:20 'a fole et a nice'; 114:18–19 'tans et hore; las et traveillié'), but rather than being stylistic padding, they betray a desire for emphasis or precision of meaning. More sophisticated rhetorical devices are used only sparingly to embellish the narrative, although they occur in greater concentration in direct speech (dialogues and monologues), where their function is to persuade an interlocutor or to move the reader. Chiasmus, the crosswise arrangement of parallel terms (ABBA), confers elegance and harmony on the prose (*69*, p.379) and is employed most poignantly to record the deaths of Arthur and Mordred: 'Einsi ocist li peres le fill, et li filz navra le pere a mort' (191:1–2; cf. 26:6–8, 41–43; 50:81–82). A rare metaphor is used by Arthur in describing Gawain as the 'peres et escuz' of his men (173:41) while the Roman dead are compared to 'bestes mues' (161:10; cf. 12:7–8, 198:25–26). Anaphora (repetition of a term at the beginning of successive clauses) can be seen in the recurrence of *meint* in 181:45–51 quoted above, in Gawain's lament for Gaheriet (100:49–56) and in the demoiselle d'Escalot's emphatic account of Lancelot's qualities (26:41–43). The personification of abstract ideas is rare, exemplified by Nouvele (105:15), a descendant of Latin Fama, and by Fortune, whose role is thematically significant (see Chapter 3).

The narrative style is characterised above all by irony and antithesis. Irony is employed to comic and tragic effect. Dramatic irony, whereby the reader has greater knowledge than the protagonist(s), is used humorously when Gawain insists (by repeating the phrase 'vos di veraiement', 30:76–78) that Lancelot does not love the queen. We are amused too when Gawain and Gaheriet seek the unknown knight in order to introduce him to himself (23:23–31).

Arthur's smile, indicating that he knows the truth about Lancelot's incognito, creates a bond of complicity with the reader, for the king, unlike his knights, is not in this case a victim of dramatic irony (24:7–12). However, other ironic situations are less humorous and contribute to the tragedy. Thus Arthur's confidence in Lancelot's loyalty (6:21–29) is misplaced; Gawain's willingness to defend Lancelot in combat against accusations of adultery (30:90–97) becomes ironic in the light of later events, and Arthur's desire to take Morgan back to Camelot as a companion for the queen (50:68–73) illustrates the tragi-comic misconceptions held by Arthurian characters. More pathetic still is Gawain's belief that the mourning over his brothers is on account of the queen (100:2–4). Here the adverb 'veraiement' (100:2–3) is used ironically, as was the phrase 'savoir veraiement' in relation to Arthur's trust in Lancelot (6:25). Paragraphs 6–7 illustrate well the rhetorical elaboration of the theme of knowing the truth, with annomination on *voir/verité/veraiement, savoir/ croire/ cuidier* and the antithesis *voir/ mençonge* underlining the difficult, often ironic, situation facing the protagonists.

A further type of irony is the verbal irony employed by characters who repeat a key term sarcastically, humorously or with a hint of pathetic resignation (24:9–12; 57:5–7; 74:96–101; 77:22–23, 30–31; see 69, p.375). The juxtaposition of two antithetical ideas or terms within narrative or direct speech also has the effect of increasing the tragic irony of the protagonists' situation, often marking their fall from success to disaster: 'Car si li rois vos a jusques ci amé plus que nul home, de tant vos haïra il plus' (90:88–90); 'Sire, se vos avez perdu Lancelot par ma folie, si le recouvrez par vostre savoir' (166:4–5, here Gawain admits his fault but his advice sadly goes unheeded). Moreover, verbal antithesis can underline the basic, unresolvable conflicts between the protagonists, for what pleases Arthur distresses Lancelot: 'Et si il furent assés plus lié qu'il ne soloient estre et plus joiant, cil del chastel furent plein de lermes et dolent, ausi li povre comme li riche; et savés vous pour coi il estoient si dolant?' (118:103–07). The elaborate antithesis here is unusual for passages of narrative. Yet in including rhetoric and a

Direct Speech

Monologues in the *Mort* are not designed to deliberate on a course of action but to express feeling or regret. Most are laments full of pathos. In Lancelot's farewell to Logres (§123) the combination of exclamatory language, apostrophe (addressing an inanimate object), repetition, antithesis, binomials and hyperbole is deeply moving. This is surpassed in intensity, however, by Gawain's lament over Gaheriet (100:49–62) with its anaphoric repetition of 'biaus (douz) frere', its rhetorical questions, curses and death wishes overtaking in pathos even Arthur's outpouring of grief (99:23–29).

Dialogue is employed in the *Mort* with considerable subtlety to convey character and emotional states, to express conflict and to debate important issues, while developing the work's key themes. Paragraphs 30–36 consist of lively exchanges in which Arthur, Girflet and Gawain indulge in gossip, resulting in Guinevere's discovery of Lancelot's apparent infidelity with the demoiselle. The dialogue in which Gawain and Arthur humorously try to outdo each other regarding the identity of the anonymous knight at the Winchester tournament, is realistically convincing:

> 'Sire, savez vos qui li chevaliers est qui a veincu ceste assemblee de Wincestre...? — Por quoi le demandez vos? fet li rois. — Por ce, fet messire Gauvains, que ge ne cuit pas que vos le sachiez. — Si sai bien, fet li rois, mes vos ne le savez pas.' (30:26–33)

When Gawain is interrogated by Guinevere on the tournament his replies are beautifully ambiguous, the knight clearly unwilling to lie outright or to reveal Lancelot's secret (31:10–31). Girflet tells her the truth, yet it is Gawain's gossipping and his pleasure in the revelation of his superior knowledge (conveyed by a smile, 35:8; cf. 24:8) which lead to the queen's discovery of the identity of Lancelot's 'beloved', and to her consequent turmoil. Not only are the characters brought to life in this section through credible dialogue; the preponderance of speech also emphasises thematically the dangers inherent in an Arthurian pastime pursued in the absence of real adventures (note how gossips and eavesdroppers spend their time near windows (35:1–2; 36:1–2)). Careless talk and faulty reasoning (for example when Gawain draws false conclusions from the evidence of the demoiselle's affection for Lancelot) contribute to the tragedy.

The conversation between Bohort and Guinevere in §59 is highly rhetorical, expertly portraying character, mood and further developing the work's themes (see *61*). Guinevere's short responses to Bohort's lengthy arguments convey the queen's angry obstinacy; she has become the *belle dame sans merci* who refuses to forgive Lancelot. Yet because her jealousy is born of love, her punishment of her lover is self-destructive. So her final words are full of pathos and psychologically convincing (59:85–90). If Guinevere represents emotion, Bohort embodies reason. His speech employs all the techniques of persuasive rhetoric. At first he attempts to assuage her anger and appeals to her sense of responsibility, for if her rejection leads to Lancelot's death, the whole kingdom will suffer. He then tries to shame the queen into relenting. Appealing like a scholastic philosopher to his authorities (biblical and pagan history), he lists the examples traditionally found in misogynistic literature of men brought down by women. These *exempla* have a two-fold effect:

1. to praise Lancelot, who shares the beauty of Absolom, the wisdom of Solomon, the strength of Sampson, the chivalric prowess of Hector and Achilles (representing both sides in the Trojan war) and the loyalty in love of Tristan (an example, within the fiction of the *Mort*, taken from recent Arthurian history).
2. to criticise Guinevere, a daughter of Eve worse than Tamar, the Queen of Sheba, Delilah, Helen of Troy and Iseut. However, anyone familiar with their stories knows that Tamar and Iseut were innocent victims of love/lust, and that Bohort's words are therefore unfair. This prompts us to consider how far the author shares the knight's misogyny. Bohort, temporarily in keeping with his persona in the

Queste, disapproves of courtly love and regrets the day that Fortune ever brought the lovers together (59:15). Ironically, however, he is forced to argue for the continuation of the adultery in order to preserve Lancelot and the realm. Unable to hide his disapproval of Guinevere, he naïvely expects his criticisms to make her relent. In fact he fails, probably because he lacks sensitivity, which is evident when he suggests to Lancelot that absence will make Guinevere's heart grow fonder, so he should go off tourneying and enjoy himself (§60). Clearly Bohort does not understand lovers. If the author is gently ridiculing him or at least emphasising, through Bohort's failure to convince, the difference in ideology between the didactic *Queste* and the courtly *Mort*, the beautiful eulogy of Lancelot contained in his cousin's speech is not treated ironically. It is characterised by lyrical hyperbole, reinforced by several metaphors: Lancelot is clothed in virtue, of which Guinevere will divest him (note the antithesis 'vestuz et couverz': 'despoilleroiz...desnueroiz'); he is the sun among the stars, his demise removing from the stars (his fellow knights) their source of light (inspiration to fight); he is the flower of chivalry (59:74–78). Thus while the author's attitude towards Guinevere and Bohort is debatable, their dialogue no doubt giving rise to audience debate, his admiration for Lancelot is unquestionable. Psychologically convincing character portrayal and the discussion of ideas are thus elegantly married in this dialogue.

Characterisation

Although its characters lack physical definition, and are sometimes described with exaggeration (either to praise or vilify), the *Mort* contains some realistic and individualising details to nuance its characterisation. No medieval romance is realistic by modern standards, but although there is little investigation into motives by an omniscient narrator and few monologues conveying the inner life of characters, the author nevertheless displays a concern for psychological *vraisemblance* (verisimilitude). For example, Arthur's worries over the adultery are portrayed through sleepless nights (§7), Guinevere's love plausibly turns to jealous anger (§§32–34), and Gawain teases Bohort over the wounding of Lancelot (§46).

There are occasions, however, when psychological consistency is sacrificed to the author's need to make a point, and then the characters become more functional, vehicles for the presentation of ideas or ideals rather than three-dimensional, plausible individuals. Zuurdeeg (*158*, p.15) notes how Arthur, on first hearing of Lancelot's betrayal, is inconsistent in his response (§6). Initially, he rejects the accusation, then suggests that if Lancelot committed adultery with Guinevere it was because of the irresistible 'force d'amors' (6:27). Moreover, his calm, passive response to the news and to Agravain's proposal of a plot to catch the lovers is unconvincing. Zuurdeeg's conclusion is that Arthur is being used to express the conflict of love and honour which Lancelot's behaviour raises: we are thereby made aware of the exonerating circumstances of Lancelot's love, but also of the different influences on the king's judgement: love for his best knight, desire to keep any private shame covered up, but pressure from his family to avenge their public dishonour. We therefore need to look beyond mere psychology when elucidating the text.

This interpretation does not, however, exclude the possibility of a more psychologically consistent reading. Arthur, like other elderly statesmen of medieval literature, is portrayed as being slow to anger and unwilling to respond to accusations which at this stage are unproven. His knowledge of Lancelot's loyalty to him indicates that Agravain's words are lies, hence his non-committal 'do as you wish'. The narrator then makes Arthur's position clear: he is kept awake thinking about the assertion, but is not willing to believe it easily 'legierement' (7:2–3). Nevertheless, he puts the lovers to the test, expecting to prove Agravain's 'mençonge' (7:13). The demoiselle d'Escalot episode allays all suspicion until Morgan's revelations. Some critics accuse Arthur of implausibility, even amnesia, when he greets her words and Agravain's further denunciations of Lancelot (§86) with 'surprise' (see *65*, pp.133–34). In fact, Arthur's response to the pictorial evidence and Morgan's speech is carefully worded. At first he is 'touz esbahiz et touz trespansez' (52:4), not surprised so much as shocked and thrown into turmoil. Then he realises that he has visual proof (53:20–22; cf. 30:97–102), and after much reflection admits that this confirms Agravain's words. His resolution to wreak revenge on Lancelot, should he catch him with Guinevere (53:59–81), is tempered however by the hypothetical conditions his speech contains — he still accepts the possibility that the evidence presented by this marvellous castle (48:75–82) is unreliable. On his return to Camelot, where Lancelot's absence seems to belie the adultery, Arthur's psychological state is again described with some subtlety: 'assez fu ses cuers en diverses pensees' (62:6–7). Although he dismisses the accusations, there is a marked development in his thinking, for whereas before he rejected the rumours as lies, from now on he is suspicious of the queen (62:14–16). His later response to Agravain, 'Si mue couleur et devint pales, et dist: "Ce sont merveilles"' (86:32–33), expresses distress rather than astonishment. Thus Arthur does not suffer from amnesia nor repression of the truth; instead the author describes plausibly the evolving mental anguish of a just king who is torn by conflicting evidence and allegiances.

Structure and Meaning

The complexities of interpreting the *Mort* are enhanced by its sophisticated structure. Devices such as interlace, juxtaposition, gradation, repetition, analogy, parallelism and doubling are employed for functional and aesthetic reasons: to convey meaning and to create a well-proportioned work.

The first third of the *Mort* (until §85) is dominated by the interlacing of two narrative threads which focus on the heroes Arthur and Lancelot. The interlace is signalled by formulae stating that the *conte* (which appears to narrate itself) is leaving one character to relate simultaneous events befalling another. The effect of this strategy is to fragment the narrative viewpoint, to facilitate dramatic irony and to defer the inevitable confrontation between Arthur and Lancelot over the queen. This section recalls the *Lancelot* proper with its proliferation of narratives which defy closure, and it is characterised by repetition. Tournaments, quests for an unknown knight, woundings, misunderstandings, mysterious knights and squires encountered in the forest, a hospitable host with a beautiful daughter (offering hospitality first to Lancelot, then to Gawain) are hallmarks of romance at its most fecund, although these events turn out to be pale reflections of the real Arthurian adventures undertaken prior to the Grail quest.

At the level of characterisation the *entrelacement* renders the conflict in Arthur's mind more plausible, for while we the readers have knowledge of both narrative strands, the king suffers from the fragmentation of reality which the labyrinthine narrative reflects. Interlace thus creates dramatic irony (see *49*). However, the *Mort* contains another kind of narrative irony, for while Lancelot and Guinevere suffer separation (mirrored in the *conte*'s separation of their narrative threads), first because of Lancelot's wounds, then because of Guinevere's jealous anger, their adulterous love is preserved. Only when they are reconciled and their narratives merge is their love finally doomed. This occurs in §85, one of several pivotal paragraphs in which one strand of the tale is resolved and another is announced (cf. §§62 & 119). In §85 the poisoned fruit and demoiselle d'Escalot episodes are completed, yet the lovers' conversation about the demoiselle's fated love seems to inspire *folie* in them, for the author immediately narrates the result of their indiscretion: discovery by the king's nephews and a further attempt to catch them red-handed (85:33 ff). As we saw in Chapter 2, once Arthur's nephews have been killed during Lancelot's rescue of the queen, the narrative becomes more linear: the composition is tight, dramatic, moving inexorably towards the finale. Interlace is still employed, but tends to relate the *same* events from two viewpoints: the deaths of Arthur's nephews (§§94–101), the siege of Joyeuse Garde (§§108–19). At §134 the narrative splits again to relate Mordred's treachery and Arthur's pursuit of Lancelot, followed by the Roman war. However, despite references to Lancelot, from §163 onwards the narrative focuses on the struggle between father and illegitimate son, the *conte* returning to Lancelot only after Arthur's death.

Norris Lacy's study of spatial form in the *Mort* (*98*) illustrates nicely the difference in narrative structure before and after §85. The first section (§§6–30) is characterised by circularity, by an ABCBA arrangement of narrative segments as follows:

The Art of the Prose Romancer

- A. Arthur's suspicions are aroused by Agravain's accusations of adultery.
- B. Lancelot accepts the demoiselle's favour.
- C. Tournament.
- B'. Gawain learns of Lancelot's involvement with the demoiselle.
- A'. Arthur's fears are assuaged.

This pattern is then repeated in §§31–71, but acquires more complexity:

- A. Guinevere's jealousy.
- B. Death of demoiselle mentioned but not known at court (dramatic irony).
- C. Pictures at Morgan's castle arouse Arthur's suspicions.
- D. Lancelot arrives at court.
- E. Queen rejects her lover.
- D'. Lancelot departs.
- C'. King's suspicions allayed when he discovers that Lancelot has already left.
- B'. Demoiselle's body discovered.
- A'. Queen's jealousy appeased.

Omitted from this scheme are the poisoned fruit and 'accident de chasse' episodes, which are analysed below.

In the early paragraphs of the *Mort* the symmetrical, circular arrangement emphasises the temporary postponement of the protagonists' tragic fall. After §85 the structural pattern alters, the organisation of later episodes being more linear:

- A. The lovers' indiscretion leads to discovery.
- B. Attempt to catch them *in flagrante delicto*.
- B'. Lancelot escapes.
- C. Arthur's nephews are killed during the rescue of the queen.

- A'. The pope intervenes.
- C'. Lancelot offers reparation for the deaths.
- D. Gawain rejects his offer, fights a duel and receives a serious headwound.

Although the adultery plot is resolved, signalled by the ABB'A' order, the repercussions of the killing of Gawain's brothers (marked by the intrusion of C into the scheme) are insurmountable despite Lancelot's charitable efforts (C'). The narrative structure thus reveals that although the adultery provokes initial conflict it is not the only or primary cause of Arthur's downfall.

While there is no episode in the second half of the *Mort* that could be deemed superfluous, the first half contains some mysterious events recalling the traditional adventures of romance. One such episode is Gawain and Gaheriet's encounter with two squires carrying a dead knight (§23). The episode does not further the plot since the squires cannot supply information on the winner of the Winchester tournament. It merely develops the humorously ironic situation of Arthur's nephews seeking without success the identity of an unknown knight whom they know well. However, on a thematic level, the plight of the dead knight enhances the atmosphere of misfortune which pervades the work. Mentioned in between two episodes narrating Lancelot's wounding, the anonymous knight could be read as a reflection of the hero, the unheroic manner of his death (23:34–36) possibly an unflattering comment on the way in which Lancelot's adulterous passion and his desire for chivalric honour will cause his ruin. So while the episode may not be significant, the possibility of symbolic or analogical readings must be countenanced.

Whereas this anonymous knight is linked with the demoiselle d'Escalot and Gaheris by the theme of death, the structural devices of juxtaposition and interlace encourage a joint reading of the poisoned fruit episode and Lancelot's 'accident de chasse'. Paragraph 62, another pivotal paragraph, in which Arthur's suspicions of cuckoldry are replaced by anxiety over accusations of murder against the queen, is followed almost immediately by the narration of Lancelot's wounding (§64). Bérier (*34*) reads the hunting accident symbolically,

The Art of the Prose Romancer

seeing in the queen's lover rather implausible christological parallels. Mora (*119*), on the other hand, adopting the moral optic of the *Queste,* emphasises the sinful connotations of Lancelot's (possibly sexual) wound in the thigh and Guinevere's Eve-like behaviour. For Mora, this episode is characterised by irony (64:35–39), the audience's expectations of a heroic adventure being thwarted by an author intent on showing the workings of Providence in a world bereft of grace. Indeed, it is apposite that Lancelot be wounded by one of Arthur's huntsmen since he is sinning against the king. Although I am unconvinced by both the christological and strongly providential readings, preferring to see Guinevere and Lancelot primarily as victims of misfortune here, the juxtaposition and interlacing of these two episodes are clearly suggestive of deeper significance. Tantalising parallels challenge the reader, but the text resists definitive interpretation.

In her fine structural study of the *Mort* Zuurdeeg (*158*, pp.24–38) shows how the interlacing of the demoiselle d'Escalot and poisoned fruit episodes, both producing innocent victims, illustrates the inexorable role of *mescheance* in this final branch of the cyclic romance. The downward spiralling of the narrative is reinforced by the repetition with gradation (an increase in seriousness, hence tragic consequences) of key events: two judicial combats (the first resolved without injury, the second producing Gawain's head-wound); two attempts to trap the lovers (the first failing, the second leading to conflict). Thus the structure of the *Mort* underlines the tragic inevitability of the end of Arthurian civilisation, but also the protagonists' contribution to it (the rapid deterioration in relations between the kin of Arthur and the family of Ban mirrored by Gawain's increasing *desmesure*).

A ternary rhythm is adopted, however, for the emotional and lyric highpoint of the work: Arthur's discovery of the bodies of his three nephews (§§98–99). Beginning with the least favourite nephew, Agravain, Arthur then finds Guerrehet and Gahieret, his lamenting growing in intensity and pathos. In contrast, after the choral repetition of 'Missire Gauvain, se vos voulez veoir vostre grant duel' (100:6–7; 100:19–20) echoed by Arthur (100:27–28), the gradation adopts a descending order as Gawain is first shown his favourite brother's body (§100), then the other two (§101).

Further examples of repetition are the predictions of war and prophecies of doom which grow in frequency as the work progresses. Again, these underline the impossibility of escaping one's fate (see *158*, Chapter IV). However, repetition can be accompanied by significant variation. So Gawain, who at first refuses to reveal the adulterous liaison and punish Lancelot, predicting a dreadful war should the secret be known, later pursues revenge against Lancelot, thus precipitating ironically the very war he hoped to avoid. The author thereby opposes two conceptions of honour: for Gawain it is acceptable for the king to be cuckolded in private (85:42–76), but unacceptable for his nephews to remain publicly unavenged (110:10–22).

Another device which encourages comparative readings is parallelism, although again similarity can highlight significant differences too. As we saw in Chapter 4, the linking of adultery and killing through the parallel treatment of the adulterers as murderers (Lancelot and Guinevere both being falsely accused of murder) creates rather than resolves any moral ambiguity. Likewise, parallels between Mordred's and Lancelot's desire for Guinevere are complicated by the important distinguishing factor that Lancelot has no desire to usurp the throne. For Delcourt (*62*, p.46) Fortune's prediction of disaster in Arthur's dream is analogous to Morgan's revelation of the adultery. In both cases women convey 'the truth' through dialogue and pictures, but in Delcourt's view only the truth of Fortune acting for Providence is valid, for Morgan's truth is deceitful, concentrating exclusively on the negative facts about Arthur's otherwise loyal knight. While it is debatable whether Fortune is unequivocally providential (see Chapter 3), Delcourt's comparative reading is fruitful in that it uncovers the moral relativism of the *Mort*. In the absence of narratorial comment we are left to interpret these parallels, the differences only adding to the ambiguity of the work.

It is clear from recent scholarship that the structural patterns in the *Mort*, while aesthetically pleasing, are not designed to impose

The Art of the Prose Romancer

one authoritative interpretation on the work. Events are not subordinated to a single overriding message, they are organised paratactically (i.e. juxtaposed) and this parataxis (a preference for co-ordination over subordination) is evident even in the text's sentence structure. At every level of the narration it is up to the reader to supply causality and discover meaning. Thus we mimic the protagonists in their search for certainties, values and possible explanations.

6. Conclusion

The *Mort* treats the universal themes of love, power and death in a specifically medieval setting of warfare and feudal society. From it we learn much about the concerns and ideals of thirteenth-century French clerics and nobles, and are moved by its depiction of the tragic death of their most famous literary hero. However, the *Mort* also treats the subject of writing and reading. The text embodies a desire to record Arthurian (hi)story, illustrated by Lancelot's *bande dessinée*, the numerous epitaphs, inscriptions and the role of Arthur's clerks to commemorate (i.e. to commit to lasting memory) the deeds of the Knights of the Round Table. In the Vulgate Cycle the presence of a narrator (commenting on the action and conveying a sense of authorial control over the material) is minimised, his role filled by the autonomous *conte*. In the absence of a guiding voice to help us interpret the text, the reader joins the protagonists on their quest for understanding. So just as the *Mort* is about writing, it is also and more importantly about reading. Characters are constantly engaged in interpreting signs, be it Arthur contemplating Lancelot's pictures or Fortune's wheel, or protagonists questioning external evidence and ultimately their own fates. This final branch of the Vulgate Cycle shows that the key values of Arthurian society: love, loyalty, honour, truth are not absolutes, for absolutes exist only in the next world. This is for me the primary meaning of the *Mort Artu*.

Bibliography

The following bibliography contains works referred to in the text and a few useful items not mentioned specifically. Students requiring a preliminary reading list on the *Mort* should consult the critical works asterisked.

EDITIONS AND TRANSLATIONS OF THE VULGATE CYCLE

1. *La Mort le roi Artu: roman du XIIIe siècle*, ed. Jean Frappier (Paris: Droz, 1936).
2. **La Mort le roi Artu: roman du XIIIe siècle*, ed. Jean Frappier, 3rd edn, TLF 58 (Geneva: Droz/Paris: Minard, 1964).
3. *La Mort du roi Arthur*, trans. Marie-Louise Ollier, 10/18 (Paris: UGE, 1992).
4. *La Mort du Roi Arthur*, trans. Monique Santucci (Paris: Champion, 1991).
5. *The Death of King Arthur*, trans. James Cable (Harmondsworth: Penguin, 1971).
6. Kunstmann, Pierre and Martin Dubé, *Concordance analytique de la 'Mort le roi Artu'*, 2 vols (Ottawa: Editions de l'Université d'Ottawa, 1982).
7. *La Queste del Saint Graal*, ed. Albert Pauphilet, CFMA (Paris: Champion, 1923).
8. *The Quest of the Holy Grail*, trans. Pauline Matarasso (Harmondsworth: Penguin, 1969).
9. *Lancelot: roman en prose du XIIIe siècle*, ed. Alexandre Micha, TLF, 9 vols (Geneva: Droz, 1978–83).
10. *The Vulgate Version of the Arthurian Romances*, ed. H. Oskar Sommer, 7 vols plus index (Washington: The Carnegie Institute, 1909–16).
11. *Lancelot-Grail: the Old French Arthurian vulgate and post-vulgate in translation*, trans. Norris Lacy et al., 5 vols (New York: Garland, 1993–96).

OTHER TEXTS

12. Aristotle, *Poetics*, in *Aristotle, Horace, Longinus: classical literary criticism*, trans. T.S. Dorsch (Harmondsworth: Penguin, 1965).
13. Beroul, *Roman de Tristran*, in *Tristan et Iseut: les poèmes français, la saga norroise*, ed. and trans. Daniel Lecroix and Philippe Walter, Lettres gothiques (Paris: L.G.F., 1989).
14. Boethius, *Consolation of Philosophy*, trans. V.E. Watts (Harmondsworth: Penguin, 1969).
15. Chrétien de Troyes, *Erec et Enide*, ed. and trans. Jean-Marie Fritz, Lettres gothiques (Paris: L.G.F., 1992).
16. —, *Cligès*, ed. and trans. Charles Méla and Olivier Collet, Lettres gothiques (Paris: L.G.F., 1994).
17. —, *Le Chevalier de la charrette*, ed. and trans. Charles Méla, Lettres gothiques (Paris: L.G.F., 1992).
18. —, *Le Chevalier au lion*, ed. and trans. David Hult, Lettres gothiques (Paris: L.G.F., 1994).
19. —, *Le Conte du Graal*, ed and trans. Charles Méla, Lettres gothiques (Paris: L.G.F., 1990).
20. *The Didot Perceval According to the Manuscripts of Modena and Paris*, ed. William Roach (Philadelphia: University of Pennsylvania Press, 1941). References are to MS E (Modena).
21. *The Romance of Perceval in Prose: a translation of the E manuscript of the 'Didot Perceval'*, trans. Dell Skeels (Seattle: University of Washington Press, 1961).
22. Geoffrey of Monmouth, *The History of the Kings of Britain*, trans. Lewis Thorpe (Harmondsworth: Penguin, 1966), Arthurian section, pp.212–61.
23. *Lancelot do lac: the non-cyclic Old French prose romance*, ed. Elspeth Kennedy, 2 vols (Oxford: Clarendon Press, 1980).
24. Wace, *Roman de Brut*, in *La Geste d'Arthur*, ed. and trans. Emmanuèle Baumgartner and Ian Short, 10/18 (Paris: U.G.E., 1993).

CRITICAL WORKS

a. *Collections of essays*

25. **La Mort le roi Artu*, ed. Emmanuèle Baumgartner, Parcours critique (Paris: Klincksieck, 1994).
26. **La Mort du roi Arthur ou le crépuscule de la chevalerie*, ed. Jean Dufournet (Paris: Champion, 1994).

27. *The Lancelot-Grail Cycle: text and transformations*, ed. William W. Kibler (Austin: University of Texas Press, 1994).

b. *Individual Studies*

28. *Adler, Alfred, 'Problems of Aesthetic Versus Historical Criticism in *La Mort le roi Artu*', *Publications of the Modern Languages Association of America*, 65 (1950), 930–43.
29. Andrieux-Reix, Nelly, 'D'amour, de vérité, de mort: signes et enseignes', in 26, pp.9–24.
30. Archibald, Elizabeth, 'Arthur and Mordred: variations on an incest theme', *Arthurian Literature*, 8 (1989), 1–27.
31. Bastide, Mario, '*La Mort le roi Artu*, roman de l'obstination et du gâchis', in 26, pp.219–40.
32. Baumgartner, Emmanuèle, 'Figures du destinateur: Salomon, Arthur, le roi Henri d'Angleterre', in *Anglo-Norman Anniversary Essays*, ed. Ian Short (London: Anglo-Norman Text Society, 1993), pp.1–10.
33. —, 'Lancelot et le royaume', in 26, pp.25–44.
34. Bérier, François, 'Empoisonnement et accident de chasse dans *La Mort le roi Artu*: une double méprise', *Travaux de Linguistique et de Littérature*, 17 (1979), 7–22, repr. in 25, pp.86–99.
35. Blaess, Madeleine, 'Predestination in some Thirteenth-Century Prose Romances', in *Currents of Thought in French Literature: essays in memory of G.T. Clapton*, ed. T.V. Benn et al. (Oxford: Blackwell, 1965), pp.3–19.
36. Blake, H., 'Etude sur les structures narratives dans *La Mort Artu*', *Revue Belge de Philologie et d'Histoire*, 50 (1972), 733–43.
37. *Bloch, R. Howard, 'From Grail Quest to Inquest: the death of King Arthur and the birth of France', *Modern Language Review*, 69 (1974), 40–55, repr. in 25, pp.107–24.
38. —, 'The Death of King Arthur and the Waning of the Feudal Age', *Orbis Litterarum*, 29 (1974), 291–305.
39. *—, 'The Text as Inquest: form and function in the pseudo-Map cycle', *Mosaic*, 8 (1975), 107–19.
40. —, *Medieval French Literature and Law* (Berkeley: California University Press, 1977).
41. Bogdanow, Fanni, 'The Changing Vision of Arthur's Death', in *Dies Illa: death in the Middle Ages*, ed. Jane H.M. Taylor (Liverpool: Francis Cairns, 1984), pp.107–23.
42. —, 'La Chute du royaume d'Arthur: évolution d'un thème', *Romania*, 108 (1986), 504–19.
43. —, 'Robert de Boron's Vision of Arthurian History', *Arthurian Literature*, 14 (1996), 19–52.

44. Bouché, Thérèse, 'De Chrétien de Troyes à la *Mort le roi Artu*: le personnage d'Arthur ou la désagrégation progressive d'un mythe', *Op. cit.*, 3 (1994), 5–13.
45. Boutet, Dominique, 'Sur l'origine et le sens de la largesse arthurienne', *Le Moyen Age*, 89 (1983), 397–411.
46. —, 'Carrefours idéologiques de la royauté arthurienne', *Cahiers de Civilisation Médiévale*, 28 (1985), 3–17, repr. in *25*, pp.125–42.
47. —, *Charlemagne et Arthur ou le roi imaginaire* (Paris: Champion, 1992).
48. —, 'Arthur et son mythe dans *La Mort le Roi Artu*: visions psychologique, politique et théologique', in *26*, pp.45–65.
49. Brandsma, Frank, '"Et la roine...s'en sourist": dramatic irony and the narrative technique of interlace', *Neophilologus*, 73 (1989), 339–49.
50. Bruce, J., 'The Development of the Mort Arthur Theme in Mediaeval Romance', *Romanic Review*, 4 (1913), 403–71.
51. —, *The Evolution of Arthurian Romance*, 2 vols, 2nd ed. repr. (Gloucester, Massachussetts: Peter Smith, 1958).
52. Bührer-Thierry, Geneviève, 'La Reine adultère', *Cahiers de Civilisation Médiévale*, 35 (1992), 299–312.
53. Burns, Jane, *Arthurian Fictions: rereading the Vulgate Cycle* (Columbus: Ohio State University Press, 1985).
54. Busby, Keith, *Gawain in Old French Literature* (Amsterdam: Rodopi, 1980).
55. Carman, J. Neale, *A Study of the 'Pseudo-Map Cycle' of Arthurian Romance* (Lawrence: University of Kansas Press, 1973).
56. Chase, Carol, '"Or dist li contes": narrative interventions and the implied audience in the *Estoire del Saint Graal*', in *27*, pp.117–38.
57. Chênerie, Marie-Luce, 'Le Motif de la *merci* dans les romans arthuriens des XIIe et XIIIe siècles', *Le Moyen Age*, 83 (1977), 5–52.
58. —, 'Preudome dans *La Mort Artu*: étude sémantique et stylistique', in *26*, pp.67–83.
59. Clough, Andrea 'Medieval Tragedy and the Genre of *Troilus and Criseyde*', *Medievalia et Humanistica*, 11 (1982), 211–27.
60. Colliot, Régine, 'Les Epitaphes arthuriennes', *Bulletin Bibliographique de la Société Internationale Arthurienne*, 25 (1973), 155–75, repr. in *25*, pp.148–62.
61. *Croizy-Naquet, Catherine, 'Le Discours de Bohort ou l'impossible dialogue avec la reine', *Op. cit.*, 3 (1994), 15–23.
62. *Delcourt, Denyse, 'La Vérité dans *La Mort le roi Artu*: couverture, détours, et labyrinthe', *Medioevo Romanzo*, 22 (1998), 16–60.
63. Dubost, Francis, 'Fin de partie: les dénouements dans *La Mort le roi Artu*', in *26*, pp.85–111.
64. Fox, Marjorie, *'La Mort le roi Artus': étude sur les manuscrits, les sources et la composition de l'oeuvre* (Paris: De Boccard, 1933).

65. Edwards, Elizabeth, 'Amnesia and Remembrance in Malory's *Morte Darthur*', *Paragraph*, 13 (1990), 132–46.
66. Frappier, Jean, 'Plaidoyer pour l'"Architecte", contre une opinion d'Albert Pauphilet sur le *Lancelot en prose*', *Romance Philology*, 8 (1954–55), 27–33.
67. *—, 'The Vulgate Cycle', in *Arthurian Literature in the Middle Ages: a collaborative history*, ed. Roger S. Loomis (Oxford: Clarendon Press, 1959), pp.295–319.
68. —, 'La Bataille de Salesbieres', in *Mélanges Rita Lejeune*, 2 vols (Gembloux: Duculot, 1969), II, 1007–23, repr. in *25*, pp.43–56.
69. *—, , *Etude sur 'La Mort le roi Artu'*, 2nd edn (Geneva: Droz, 1961).
70. *—, 'La Mort le Roi Artu', extracted from an earlier article and repr. in *25*, pp.27–38.
71. Fries, Maureen, 'Boethian Themes and Tragic Structure in Geoffrey of Monmouth's *Historia Regum Britanniae*', in *The Arthurian Tradition: essays in convergence*, ed. Mary Flowers Braswell and John Brugge (Tucsaloo: University of Alabama Press, 1988), pp. 29–42.
72. Gouttebroze, Jean-Guy, 'La Conception de Mordret dans le *Lancelot* propre et dans la *Mort le roi Artu*: tradition et originalité', in *26*, pp.113–31.
73. Grisward, Joël, 'Le Motif de l'épée jetée au lac: la mort d'Arthur et la mort de Batradz', *Romania*, 90 (1969), 289–340, 473–514, final part repr. in *25*, pp.57–75.
74. Guerin, M. Victoria, 'The King's Sin: the origins of the David-Arthur parallel', in *The Passing of Arthur*, ed. Christopher Baswell and William Sharpe (New York: Garland, 1988), pp.15–30.
75. —, *The Fall of Kings and Princes: structure and destruction in Arthurian tragedy* (Stanford: Stanford University Press, 1985).
76. Hanning, Robert, *The Vision of History in Early Britain: from Gildas to Geoffrey of Monmouth* (New York: Columbia University Press, 1966).
77. —, 'Arthurian Evangelists: the language of truth in thirteenth-century French prose romances', *Philological Quarterly*, 64 (1985), 347–65.
78. Hartman, Richard, 'Le Rôle du roturier dans *La Mort le roi Artu*', *Marche Romane*, 29 (1979), 81–91.
79. Hunt, Tony, 'Beroul's *Tristran* and Abelardian Ethics', *Romania*, 98 (1977), 501–40.
80. —, 'Character and Causality in the Oxford *Roland*', *Medioevo Romanzo*, 5 (1978), 3–33.
81. —, 'The Tragedy of Roland: an Aristotelian view', *Modern Language Review*, 74 (1979), 791–805.
82. —, *Chrétien de Troyes: 'Yvain' (Le Chevalier au lion)*, Critical Guides to French Texts 55 (London: Grant & Cutler, 1986).

83. Imbs, Paul, 'La Journée dans la *Queste del Saint Graal* et *La Mort le roi Artu*', in *Mélanges de philologie romane et de littérature médiévale offerts à E. Hoepffner* (Paris: Belles Lettres, 1949), pp.279–93.
84. Johnson, L.A., 'Commemorating the Past: a critical study of the shaping of British and Arthurian history in Geoffrey of Monmouth's *Historia regum Britanniae*, Wace's *Roman de Brut*, Lazamon's *Brut* and the alliterative *Morte Arthure* (Ph.D. London, 1990).
85. Joly, Jehanne, 'Rêves prémonitoires et fin du monde arthurien', in *Fin des temps et temps de la fin dans l'univers médiéval* (Aix-en-Provence: CUERMA, 1993), *Senefiance*, 33 (1993), 261–84.
86. *Kay, Sarah, 'Adultery and Killing in *La Mort le roi Artu*', in *Scarlet Letters: fictions of adultery from antiquity to the 1990s*, ed. Nicholas White and Naomi Segal (Basingstoke: Macmillan, 1997), 34–44.
87. Kelly, Douglas, 'Age and the Ages of Life in the *Prose Lancelot*', in *27*, pp. 51–66.
88. Kennedy, Angus, 'The Hermit's Role in French Arthurian Romance (1170–1350)', *Romania*, 95 (1974), 54–83.
89. —, 'Lancelot Incognito at Winchester in the *Mort Artu*', *Bulletin Bibliographique de la Société Internationale Arthurienne*, 27 (1975), 170–71.
90. Kennedy, Elspeth, 'King Arthur in the first part of the Prose *Lancelot*', in *Medieval Miscellany Presented to E. Vinaver* (Manchester: Manchester University Press, 1965), pp.186–95.
91. —, *Lancelot and the Grail: a study of the prose 'Lancelot'* (Oxford: Clarendon Press, 1986).
92. —, 'The Re-writing and Re-reading of a Text: the evolution of the *Prose Lancelot*', in *The Changing Face of Arthurian Romance: essays on Arthurian prose romances in memory of C. E. Pickford*, ed. Alison Adams et al. (Cambridge: Brewer, 1986), pp.1–9.
93. —, 'Failure in Arthurian Romance', *Medium Aevum*, 60 (1991), 16–32.
94. —, '"Lancelot li mescheans": mischance and individual responsibility in the *Lancelot-Grail*', in *De ongevallliche Lanceloet: studies over de Lancelotcompilatie*, ed. Bart Besamusca and Frank Brandsma (Hilversum: Verloren, 1992), pp.117–36.
95. —, 'Variations in Patterns of Interlace in the Lancelot-Grail', in *27*, pp.31–50.
96. Knapp, Fritz-Peter, 'De l'aventure profane à l'aventure spirituelle: le double Esprit du *Lancelot en prose*', *Cahiers de Civilisation Médiévale*, 32 (1989), 263–66.
97. Lachet, Claude, 'Mais où sont les tournois d'antan? La fin des joutes dans *La Mort le Roi Artu*', in *26*, pp.133–55.
98. Lacy, Norris, 'Spatial Form in the *Mort Artu*', *Symposium*, 31 (1977), 337–45, repr. in *25*, pp.100–06.
99. —, 'The *Mort Artu* and Cyclic Closure', in *27*, pp.85–97.

100. Lagorio, Valerie, 'The Apocalyptic Mode in the Vulgate Cycle of Arthurian Romances', *Philological Quarterly*, 57 (1978), 1–22.
101. Larmat, Jean, 'Les Idées morales dans *La Mort le roi Artu*', *Annales de la Faculté des Lettres et Sciences Humaines de Nice*, 2 (1967), 49–60.
102. Leech, Clifford, *Tragedy*, The Critical Idiom (London and New York: Methuen, 1969).
103. Leupin, Alexandre, *Le Graal et la littérature: étude sur la vulgate arthurienne en prose* (Lausanne: L'Age d'Homme, 1982).
104. Lindon, M., *La Tradition dans 'La Mort le roi Artu'* (Diss. Paris VII, 1979).
105. Lot, Ferdinand, *Etude sur le 'Lancelot en prose'* (1918, repr. Paris: Champion, 1954).
106. Lot-Borodine, Myrrha, 'Le Double esprit et l'unité du *Lancelot en prose*', in *Mélanges d'histoire du moyen âge offerts à F. Lot par ses amis et ses élèves* (Paris: Champion, 1925), pp.477–90.
107. *Lyons, Faith, '*La Mort le roi Artu*: an interpretation', in *The Legend of Arthur in the Middle Ages*, ed. Grout, Lodge, Pickford and Varty (Cambridge: Brewer, 1983), pp.138–48.
108. *MacRae, Donald, 'Appearances and Reality in *La Mort le roi Artu*', *Forum for Modern Language Studies*, 18 (1982), 266–77.
109. Marx, Jean, *La Légende arthurienne et le Graal* (Paris: P.U.F, 1952).
110. *Maurice, Jean, *La Mort le Roi Artu* (Paris: P.U.F, 1995).
111. Méla, Charles, *La Reine et le Graal: la conjointure dans les romans du Graal, de Chrétien de Troyes au Livre de Lancelot* (Paris: Seuil, 1984).
112. —, 'Life in *La Mort le roi Artu*', in *The Passing of Arthur*, ed. Christopher Baswell and William Sharpe (New York: Garland, 1988), pp.5–14. French version repr. in 25, pp.143–47.
113. Ménard, Philippe, 'Le Don en blanc qui lie le donateur: réflexions sur un motif de conte', in *An Arthurian Tapestry*, ed. Kenneth Varty (Glasgow: French Department of the University of Glasgow, 1981), pp. 37–53.
114. Micha, Alexandre, 'Deux Sources de la *Mort Artu*', *Zeitschrift für romanische Philologie*, 66 (1950), 369–72, repr. in 25, pp.39–42.
115. —, 'L'Esprit du Lancelot-Graal', *Romania*, 82 (1961), 357–78.
116. —, 'Sur la composition du *Lancelot en prose*', in *Etudes de langue et de littérature médiévales offertes à F. Lecoy* (Paris: Champion, 1973), pp.417–25.
117. —, *Essais sur le cycle du Lancelot-Graal* (Geneva: Droz, 1987).
118. —, 'La Géographie de *La Queste* et de *La Mort Artu*', in *Farai chansoneta novele: essais sur la liberté créatrice au moyen âge. Hommage à Jean-Charles Payen* (Caen: Centre de Publications de l'Université de Caen, 1990), pp.267–73.
119. Mora, Francine, 'L'Accident de chasse de Lancelot dans *La Mort le roi Artu*: jeux du narrateur et jeux du destin', in *Miscellanea Mediaevalia:*

mélanges offerts à Philippe Ménard, ed. Jean-Claude Faucon, Alain Labbé and Danielle Quéruel, 2 vols (Paris: Champion, 1998), II, 1007–18.

120. Morris, Rosemary, *The Character of King Arthur in Medieval Literature* (Cambridge: Brewer, 1982).
121. *Muir, Lynette and R. Howard Bloch, 'Further Thoughts on the *Mort Artu*', *Modern Language Review*, 71 (1976), 26–30.
122. *Noble, Peter, 'Some Problems in *La Mort le roi Artu*', *Modern Language Review*, 65 (1970), 519–22.
123. —, 'The Role of Fairy Mythology in *La Mort le roi Artu*', *Studi Francesi*, 15 (1971), 480–83.
124. —, 'Les Structures sociales de *La Mort le roi Artu*', in *Actes du 14ᵉ Congrès International Arthurien*, 2 vols (Rennes: Presses Universitaires de Rennes II, 1985), II, 449–55.
125. —, *Beroul's 'Tristan' and the 'Folie de Berne'*, Critical Guides to French Texts 15 (London: Grant & Cutler, 1982).
126. Ollier, Marie-Louise, 'Le Sens du procès dans La *Mort Artu*', in *26*, pp.157–79.
127. Patterson, Lee, 'The Historiography of Romance and the Alliterative *Morte Arthure*', *Journal of Medieval and Renaissance Studies*, 13 (1983), 3–32.
128. Pauphilet, Albert, Review of F. Lot, *Etude sur le Lancelot en prose*', *Romania*, 45 (1918–19), 514–34.
129. —, 'Sur la composition du *Lancelot-Graal*', in *Le Legs du moyen âge* (Melun: d'Argences, 1950), pp.212–17.
130. Pensom, Roger, 'Rapports du symbole et de la narration dans *Yvain* et dans *La Mort Artu*', *Romania*, 94 (1973), 398–416.
131. Perret, Michèle, 'Façons de dire: les verbes de parole et de communication dans *La Mort le roi Artu*', in *26*, pp.181–95.
132. Pickering, F.P., 'Notes on Fate and Fortune (for Germanisten), in *Medieval German Studies presented to Frederick Norman* (London: Institute of Germanic Studies, 1965), 1–15.
133. Planche, Alice, 'Les Mots de la mort et du malheur dans *La Mort le Roi Artu*, in *De l'aventure épique à l'aventure romanesque: hommage à André de Mandach*, ed. Jacques Chocheyras (Bern: Peter Lang, 1997), pp.269–80.
134. de Pontfarcy, Yolande, 'Source et structure de l'épisode de l'empoisonnement dans *La Mort Artu*', *Romania*, 99 (1978), 246–55.
135. *Pratt, Karen, 'Aristotle, Augustine or Boethius? *La Mort le roi Artu* as Tragedy', *Nottingham French Studies*, 30 (1991), 81–109.
136. Richards, I.A., *Principles of Literary Criticism* (London: Kegan Paul, 1926).

137. Rychner, Jean, *L'Articulation des phrases narratives dans la 'Mort Artu': formes et structures de la prose médiévale* (Geneva: Droz, 1970).
138. —, 'L'Attaque de phrase en sujet nominal + incidence + verbe dans la Mort Artu', *Revue de Linguistique Romane*, 34 (1970), 26–38.
139. Santucci, Monique, 'Propos sur la structure de *la Mort Artu*', *Travaux de Littérature*, 5 (1992), 7–17.
140. —, 'Amour, aimer dans *La Mort le roi Artu*', in *26*, pp.197–218.
141. Sargent-Baur, Barbara Nelson, '*Dux bellorum/rex militum*/roi fainéant: la transformation d'Arthur au XIIe siècle', *Le Moyen Age*, 90 (1984), 357–73.
142. Schichtman, Martin B. and Laurie A. Finke, 'Profiting from the Past: history as symbolic capital in the *Historia Regum Britanniae*', *Arthurian Literature*, 12 (1993), 1–35.
143. Segre, Cesare, 'Deconstruction and Reconstruction of a Tale: from *La Mort le roi Artu* to the novellino', in Cesare Segre, *Structures and Time* (Chicago: University of Chicago Press, 1979), pp.58–64.
144. Solterer, Helen, '"Conter le terme de cest brief": l'inscription dans *La Mort le roi Artu*', in *Actes du 14e Congrès International Arthurien*, 2 vols (Presses Universitaires de Rennes II, 1985), II, 558–68.
145. Stones, M. Alison, 'Aspects of Arthur's Death in Medieval Illumination', in *The Passing of Arthur*, ed. Christopher Baswell and William Sharpe (New York: Garland, 1988), pp. 52–101.
146. —, 'The Earliest Illustrated *Prose Lancelot* Manuscript', *Reading Medieval Studies*, 3 (1977), 3–44.
147. Suard, François, 'La Conception de l'aventure dans le *Lancelot* en prose', *Romania*, 108 (1987), 230–53.
148. *—, 'Hasard et nécessité dans *La Mort le Roi Artu*', in *De l'aventure épique à l'aventure romanesque: hommage à André de Mandach*, ed. Jacques Chocheyras (Bern: Peter Lang, 1997), pp.281–94.
149. *Szkilnik, Michelle, 'Loiauté et traïson dans la *Mort le roi Artu*', *Op. cit.*, 3 (1994), 25–32.
150. *Terry, Patricia, 'Certainties of the Heart: the poisoned fruit episode as a unifying exemplum in *La Mort le roi Artu*', *Romance Languages Annual*, 1 (1990), 328–31.
151. *Trachsler, Richard, 'Au-delà de la *Mort le roi Artu*: ce dont parle le conte quand le roi a disparu', *Op. cit.*, 3 (1994), 33–41.
152. van Emden, Wolfgang G., '*Argumentum ex Silentio*: an aspect of dramatic technique in *La Chanson de Roland*', *Romance Philology*, 43 (1989), 181–96.
153. Vinaver, Eugène, *The Rise of Romance* (Oxford: Clarendon Press, 1971).
154. Walter, Philippe, *La Mémoire du temps: fêtes et calendriers de Chrétien de Troyes à la 'Mort Artu'* (Paris: Champion, 1989).

155. —, 'La Fin du monde arthurien', in *Apogée et déclin, textes réunis par Claude Thomasset et Michel Zink* (Paris: Presses de l'Université de Paris Sorbonne, 1993), pp.155–68, repr. in *25*, pp.76–85.
156. Weill, Isabelle, 'Le Temps du futur et le temps du passé dans *la Mort le roi Artu* ou le système temporel d'un désastre annoncé', in *Fin des temps et temps de la fin dans l'univers médiéval* (Aix-en-Provence: CUERMA, 1993), *Senefiance*, 33 (1993), 536–45.
157. Zuurdeeg, Atie D., 'The Nature of Lancelot's Sin in *La Mort le roi Artu*', *Res Publica Litterarum*, 2 (1979), 359–64.
158. *—, *Narrative Techniques and their Effects in 'La Mort le roi Artu'* (York, South Carolina: French Literature Publications Co., 1981).
159. Greene, Virginie, *Le Sujet et la mort dans 'La Mort Artu'* (Saint-Genouph: Nizet, 2002).
160. Trachsler, Richard, *Clotûres du cycle arthurien* (Geneva: Droz, 1996).
161. *The Arthur of the French*, ed. Glyn Burgess and Karen Pratt (Cardiff: University of Wales Press, forthcoming).